WHITES CONFRONT RACISM

Antiracists and Their Paths to Action

Eileen O'Brien

ROWMAN & LITTLEFIELD PUBLISHERS, INC.

Lanham • Boulder • New York • Oxford

ROWMAN & LITTLEFIELD PUBLISHERS, INC.

Published in the United States of America
by Rowman & Littlefield Publishers, Inc.
4720 Boston Way, Lanham, Maryland 20706
www.rowmanlittlefield.com

12 Hid's Copse Road, Cumnor Hill, Oxford OX2 9JJ, England

British Library Cataloguing in Publication Information Available

Library of Congress Cataloging-in-Publication Data

O'Brien, 1972–
    Whites confront racism : antiracists and their paths to action / Eileen O'Brien
        p.   cm.
    Includes bibliographical references and index.
    ISBN 0-7425-1581-8 (alk. paper) — ISBN 0-7425-1582-6 (pbk. : alk. paper)
    1. Civil rights workers—United States—History—20th century.   2. Civil rights workers—United States—Biography.   3. Whites—United States—Politics and government—20th century.   4. Whites—United States—Biography.   5. African Americans—Civil rights—History—20th century.   6. Civil rights movements—United States—History—20th century.   7. Racism—United States—History—20th century.   8. United States—Race relations.   I. Title.
    E184.A1 O2   2001
    305.8′034073—dc21   2001031794

Printed in the United States of America

*To everyone in my hometown of Williamsburg, Virginia,
who gave me more of an education about racism
than any academic degree ever could.*

CONTENTS

PREFACE

I draw upon both Afrocentric and feminist theories when I state that thinking is inseparable from feeling and that my personal experience is indivisible from my experience as a researcher. As such, I want to begin by placing this work in the holistic context in which it occurred.

It goes back as early as age fifteen, when my life was altered forever by dating "outside my race." My mother and stepfather forbade me to associate with this African American person, so I began doing it behind their backs. Every month or so I would get caught and put on restriction, so my home life was in constant disarray. Still legally a child, I felt completely powerless, knowing that what I did was certainly not against the law, and feeling like I had a lot more maturity/morality than any of the adults that seemed to be around me. Although I had a few close friends, I lost many, including my very best friend, whose parents blamed my sordid influence for their own daughter's eventual interracial liaison. Her parents withdrew her from that school and paid extra to send her to another one her senior year, so she could start another "whiter" life without me or any of the African Americans she had managed to meet at our school. If I so much as tried to call or write her, she would be punished by being sent to live with her real father in another state. That year I also ended up in another state, living with my more supportive father to avoid the turmoil at home. Later, I returned to my hometown at age eighteen and lived the remainder of my senior year in high school with the financially difficult task of supporting myself. All this was because of racism, and it was rather firmly implanted in me by this point that most of the whites around me were intent on *not* noticing how unreasonable and far-reaching their racism could be.

College began my academic learning about racism. Instead of being seen as a teenager rebelling against her parents, I could finally be seen as participating in a relevant social movement for change. I was never a part of any regularly meeting organization for antiracism. There were none that I knew of—just isolated events and conferences I made sure to attend whenever possible. Throughout this whole process, I had always found my support in communities of color. I also was a victim of the "historical amnesia" about white antiracists, so my heroes were people like Malcolm X and Martin Luther King. My closest romantic and platonic friendships for ten years were mostly people of color, and I cherished the moments they would say, "You're not really white."

When I switched schools from my master's to my Ph.D. program, two major things happened. I moved to a new area, and both my new best friend and my romantic partner at the time happened to be white. I also started this research project on white antiracists. Ironically, while living as far south as I had ever been, I was meeting more white people who "got it" about racism than ever before. As I began the data analysis for this project, I found there were many other paths to becoming a white antiracist, and many more ways of being a white antiracist than I ever thought possible from my own limited experience. In discovering the breadth of white antiracisms, my personal and professional journeys came together in an amazing way.

Spiritually, I believe everything happens for a reason. I began my Ph.D. program wanting to research the effects of racial discrimination on people of color. My mentor and tireless white antiracist, Joe Feagin, suggested that I should study the white aspect of racism in some way since I had experience and insight into it. From rescuing me from a graduate program that would not support critical race studies to always providing me the quickest feedback on my work, to summer work, to vegan meals, and to swims in Poe Springs, Joe was and is a great support. While my hometown gave me my education on racism, my secondary and academic education on racism could not have been accomplished without Joe Feagin. For this, he has my immeasurable gratitude.

Many others have thumbed through this work in many different forms, and still others have provided personal support over the years it came together. This list, which could never be complete, includes: Michael Armato and Amanda Crawford, Eduardo Bonilla-Silva, Kendal Broad, Cynthia Burack, Amy DeLorenzo, Susan Eichenberger, Lara Foley, Sharon Foti, Douglas Godfrey, Jaber Gubrium, Ruth Harris, Nikitah Imani, Sharon Jacobson, F. Nwabueze Okoye, Natalie and Henry Rosillo, Constance Shehan, Naima Brown Smith, the Stronczeks (Amanda, Paulette, Rich, and Rita), Barbara Thompson, the Thorntons (Tim, Lisa, and Max), Hernan Vera, Jason Willis, and the Wynnes (Tammy, Mike, Taylor, and Devin). I would also like to thank my beloved family for their support and beaming pride. This includes my soul-supporter and sister, Kerry O'Brien, Mike and Shari O'Brien, Justin and Sarah Dovi, and my mother, Jean Kelly, who has taken an awesome journey from my high school days to full affirmation of my antiracism. The ultimate in beaming pride for me was my grandmother Helen O'Brien, and although she no longer inhabits this world, I know her spirit fueled mine. And my youngest inspiration is my goddaughter, Taylor Marie Wynne, whose little life helps me cling to the hope that the whites in our hometown will progress even a little bit from the days when her mother, the only black cheerleader on the squad, quit in part because of the way they were all talking about *me*.

In this book I talk about privileged resistance. One of the privileges I have been blessed with is that I was able to take the knowledge that began in Williamsburg, Virginia, and use it to fuel a journey to several degrees and even this book. I am unspeakably humbled as I reflect back on some of the African American people who taught me the biggest lessons by letting me into their lives. Some ended up selling their souls to the military to get an education, and others resorted to selling drugs, even out of my car and my living room. Now I am "Dr. O'Brien," an "expert" on what they always knew was there, and teaching college students about what they knew without ever going to college. I may be able to stick a few more fancy terms on it and add a few more statistics, but I am only using the knowledge they gave me by allowing me into their lives, in spite of the parents, teachers, students, and police officers who gave them hell for it. Ironically, they taught me more about whiteness than any whites ever did, and we barely talked about it. We did not have to—it was all around us. So as a privileged resistor, I want to above all thank all those who resist each and every day without fanfare or letters after their names. They are the true freedom fighters who inspired me through each of these pages.

Finally, to the thirty white antiracists whose words and lives fill these pages, the book simply would not be without you. Because of this, I will be donating all of my profits from the sales of this book to the two major antiracist organizations I studied, Anti-Racist Action and the People's Institute for Survival and Beyond. Whatever our differences, I hope all your work is always growing and making a difference somehow.

I

THE NEED FOR ALTERNATIVE
MODELS OF WHITENESS

> Luckily, there are individual non-black people who have divested
> of their racism. . . . We have yet to have a significant body of writing
> from these individuals that gives expression to how they have
> shifted attitudes and daily vigilantly resist becoming reinvested in
> white supremacy.
>
> —hooks, *Killing Rage*

In *The Autobiography of Malcolm X* (Malcolm X 1965), Malcolm X
wrote about a memorable "well-meaning" white woman he met.
After one of his speeches at her college, she actually boarded a
plane to follow him to his next destination in New York so she
could ask him a question. He recalled, "I'd never seen anyone I
ever spoke before more affected than this little white college girl."
This white woman's question to Malcolm X was, "What can I *do*?"
and his response at the time was "Nothing" (Malcolm X 1965, 286).
Several chapters (and many life experiences) later, Malcolm X re-
visited this moment in his life and expressed regret that this was
his only response. He wished he could get her name and contact
her to tell her what he had come to realize about whites' responsibility for working on racism. He asserted that "both races, as
human beings, ha[ve] the obligation, the responsibility of helping
to correct America's human problem. The well-meaning white
people . . . ha[ve] to combat, actively and directly, the racism in

other white people" (Malcolm X 1965, 375). Malcolm X was way ahead of his time here in terms of predicting a wave of critical white studies (see Hill 1997; Fine, Weis, and Wong 1997) that was only to occur many years later among whites. However, his original ambivalence about what whites could do about racism still reflects the mind-set of most of white America. While headlines about white supremacist violence are disturbingly commonplace today, there is no presence in the media of a vocal white opposition to this violence, much less to the everyday racism that does not make the headlines. We hear about the proliferation of hate groups but never about the proliferation of antihate groups. Besides shaking our heads and wringing our hands in dismay, most of white America has little else to offer in terms of a concrete action plan to keep racism from happening. In essence, a majority of us are complicit with Malcolm X's initial response of "nothing" to the white person who would ask, "What can I do?"

Nearly forty years later, the white woman's question of what she can do about racism still has relevance in American society. Because "one of the consequences of racism in our society is that those who oppose it are often marginalized" (Tatum 1994, 473), we do not often hear of solutions for racism in which whites can participate. When white Americans take the rare step of actually accepting and understanding the current levels of racism, their initial response is often guilt or despair. There is a dire need to break the silence about participatory solutions for racism, and to transform despair into action.

Those within the small white antiracist community are vocal about the silence with respect to their actions throughout time and the difficulty this creates for making change. Few people can name even five white antiracists throughout history, and this "historical amnesia" means that "few white people have role models or ways of knowing what has worked before—and not" (Thompson and White Women Challenging Racism 1997, 354). The historical amnesia not only makes it difficult for current white antiracists to know what to do, but it also forestalls the potential for more white people to join in the struggle. When learning about racism means that white racism is to blame for the evil, it makes it difficult for whites to retain a positive self-definition, especially when there are no alternative models widely available of how to be white and simultaneously to be an agent for positive change. Beverly Daniel Tatum (1994, 472) has written that this lack of published material on white antiracists presents a stumbling block in her college courses on racism:

> Do they [the students] know about white allies who spoke up, who worked for social change, who resisted racism and lived to tell about it? How did these white allies break free from the confines of the racist socialization they surely experienced to redefine themselves in this way? These are the voices that many white students are hungry to hear.

In an academic setting, Tatum invites white antiracist guest speakers in order to make up for this dearth of written material, which she argues is essential for the "restoration of hope" and displacement of despair, for students of color and whites alike. Knowledge about white antiracists is necessary for members of the activist and academic community interested in ending racism, yet this knowledge remains few and far between.

Furthermore, beyond the activist and academic communities, workplaces all over the country have begun to offer diversity, sensitivity, or multicultural training as part of their efforts to tolerate or appreciate their increasingly diverse staff and clientele. These are often geared toward helping whites understand people of color. What does it take to bring about this kind of change in the white mind? What initiated that change for white antiracist activists, and how is that sustained for them in their daily lives? Understanding this is a key piece of information for people who design these diversity trainings to have if they are truly interested in lasting change. As the United States steadily changes demographically toward the time when whites will be in the minority, improving the effectiveness of these programs is becoming increasingly important. Understanding whites who have not only come to comprehend racism but who are vocal and active about changing it will help us to grasp how to better structure these "diversity" trainings.

In pursuing the answers to these questions about the role of whites in antiracism, it will become evident that there are multiple ways of practicing antiracism for whites. Although it is widely acknowledged that there are multiple types of feminisms (e.g., liberal, radical), we do not have the same understanding of antiracism, even though racism and sexism are often compared as similar oppressions. Specifically, the antiracist organizations to which white antiracist activists belong are an important part of the variation among ways of doing antiracism.[1] Yet even where organizations are not a part of white antiracists' identities, there continue to be varieties of ways in which antiracism is done among them. So for those who ask the question "What can I do [about racism]?" there is an abundance of answers. It is my goal in this book to make that variety of answers available to the reader, through my own voice and the voices of other contemporary white antiracists.

WHO IS A WHITE ANTIRACIST? DEFINING TERMS

When the word "feminist" is uttered, most people at least conjure up an image of someone or something focused on rejecting sexism. Certainly, there are many different images of feminists in American popular culture—from the most radical "bra-burners" or "male bashers" to the more liberal supporters of "women's issues." Volumes have been written on the varieties of feminisms and the images and stereotypes associated with the word "feminist." Everyone from politicians to academics draws parallels between sexism and racism, so one might expect that a word like "antiracist" might be equally familiar. Yet I have lost count of how often I have had to explain the topic of my research—"white antiracists"—to people who inquire about it. Hearing the words "white" and "racist" in the same breath, especially if the word "activist" is included as a descriptor, people have tended to picture a white Ku Klux Klan or neo-Nazi activist when I have told them the topic of my research. Not only is the word "antiracist" not easily recognizable, but the coupling of the word "white" with "antiracist" makes for an even more unfamiliar designation. Who are we talking about here?

Antiracists, quite simply, are people who have committed themselves, in thought, action and practice, to dismantling racism. In our culture, "I'm not a racist" rolls off the tongues of many people, often right before they make incredibly derogatory or racially stereotypic remarks, so it is important to distinguish between "nonracists" and "antiracists." Joe Barndt has written: "Nonracists try to deny that the prison exists. Antiracists work for the prison's eventual destruction" (1991, 65). Rather than trying to minimize the significance of racism in the United States, for themselves and others, antiracists make it a point to notice and address racism regularly. I also borrow from bell hooks [sic] to develop this definition: a white antiracist is someone who "daily vigilantly resist[s] becoming reinvested in white supremacy" (1995, 157–158). So in saying that an antiracist notices and addresses racism regularly, I mean that this effort is daily and vigilant. As I sought people to interview for this research, I made them aware of this definition and relied upon their own self-definitions. For the whites whose names (or pseudonyms) appear here, being an "antiracist" by the above definition was an important part of their identities. To find out what whites can do about racism today, one of the best places to look for answers is in the lives of those who now practice antiracism as an ongoing, vigilant part of their day.

Although I have been using the terms "racism" and "white supremacy" interchangeably thus far, it is important to discuss their meanings, since racism and white supremacy (and their elimination) are the daily focus of an antiracist identity. Racism and white supremacy should not be confused, in and of themselves, with the ideology and practices of the Ku Klux Klan or other extremists. Although such an overt and even hostile stance of white racial superiority is indeed racist and white supremacist, it is only one of many dimensions of racism or white supremacy. Racism and white supremacy are manifested in blatant ways, but they also work in covert and subtle ways, and the latter are much more common in today's society than the former. Tatum (1997) has defined racism as a system of advantage, and for the duration of the United States's history that system of advantage has legally, politically, socially, and economically favored white Americans. So, certainly, any clear act of prejudice or discrimination—someone who says whites are naturally more intelligent than blacks or black homeseekers who are denied a mortgage due to their race—would be an example of racism. However, subtle and unintended actions might also be considered examples of racism, such as a television network which does not feature any actors of color in its prime time shows. So racism is a system of many different beliefs and practices (individual and institutional, intentional and unintentional)[2] which result in a collective advantage of one "race" over another.

That advantaged race has always been the white in our society, which is why people like bell hooks and others prefer the term "white supremacy" instead of racism. Because racism is often thought of as a "black problem," using the term white supremacy instead of racism shifts the focus towards whites' advantages and away from people of color's disadvantages (and also away from any advantages individual people of color may have over individual whites). The term white supremacy also reminds us that white advantage can be bolstered even when people of color are not present or not even mentioned—when "race" seems to not be an issue. Because my definition of the term "racism" includes the focus on systemic white advantages which "white supremacy" seeks to incorporate, I will be using them both interchangeably throughout this work.

The final note that should be made about definitions is that to be "white," or any "race" for that matter, is a social and cultural construct that has no true basis in biology, and is fairly recent in human history. Whole volumes have also been devoted to this idea, so I will not belabor it here except to paraphrase W. I. Thomas— even though the concepts of "black," "white," or any other "race" are not real, they are real in their consequences. It is in that spirit that I use any racial category throughout this work.

CONTINUING IN A LONG HISTORY OF WHITE ANTIRACISM

It is not just Malcolm X who once told one white person there was "nothing" she could do about racism. The very word "racism" itself often evokes images of people of color and not whites, which is why several writers have chosen to use the term "white supremacy" instead, to challenge the notion that "racism" has nothing to do with white people. There are few conversations I remember more vividly from my youth than my mother's admonishment of "Why don't you let the people who are fighting for that cause [people of color] fight for it?" when I brought my first poster of Martin Luther King, Jr., home. It is seldom nourished or supported in our culture for whites to become so dedicated to antiracism; in fact, they are discouraged constantly from doing so. The importance of establishing an alternative cultural stock of knowledge—one which boldly attests to the presence of whites in antiracist struggles as both appropriate and necessary—cannot be underscored enough.

Although certainly several writers have bemoaned the lack of a clear white presence in our collective memories of antiracist history, white involvement in antiracism is as long-standing as the United States itself. Herbert Aptheker's (1992) work *Antiracism in U.S. History: The First Two Hundred Years* traced the activities of white antiracists from the nation's beginnings up to Emancipation. He demonstrated that as early as the 1700s white and black servants were recorded as "escaping" together, and in the early 1800s the names are too numerous to list here of all the whites who were punished in some way for their roles in slave escapes or rebellions. The punishments these whites received included a hundred lashes, being tarred and feathered, being jailed, and even hanged. Although John Brown is the best-known white martyr of this period, there were several other such figures. For example, Joseph Wood was hanged in Louisiana in 1812, and George Boxley's leadership of a slave rebellion in 1816 earned him ample jail time. Whites took an active role in the establishment of antislavery societies in the early 1800s, so it is no wonder that some contemporary white antiracists have followed in this tradition by calling themselves the "New Abolitionists" (Ignatiev and Garvey 1996).

As with the civil rights movement of the 1960s, the antiracist activism of the 1800s also had strong religious roots. The white Quakers were quite involved with abolition and the Underground Railroad, and the white founder of Methodism, John Wesley, also spoke out against slavery. Names like William Lloyd Garrison, Lydia Maria Child, Thomas Garrett, Reverend Samuel J. May, and Sarah and Angelina Grimké are just a few better known names in a much longer list of whites who were actively antiracist during this time period. Their efforts were often driven by moral convictions that all humans were equal under God. Although racist and paternalistic attitudes were not absent from white abolitionist efforts, several white groups, including the Liberty Party of the 1840s, made it explicit that the abolition of slavery was but one of a list of changes that needed to be made in society to secure human rights for all citizens regardless of race (Aptheker 1992).

With the death of black abolitionist Frederick Douglass, the accommodationist politics of Booker T. Washington began to take center stage in the early 1900s. The National Association for the Advancement of Colored People (NAACP) emerged around this time as a more radical alternative to this Washingtonian strategy. Richard Thomas's (1996) book *Understanding Interracial Unity*, which also highlights the United States's long tradition of antiracism, points out that whites were present even in the earliest incarnations of the NAACP. For example, over the course of many years Mary White Ovington served as secretary, treasurer, and board member of the NAACP until her retirement in 1947. From 1911 to 1940, white lawyer Arthur B. Springarn served as vice president of the NAACP and was engaged in the struggle for antilynching laws. The Congress for Racial Equality (CORE), founded in 1942, also had white involvement from the beginning. As with the abolitionists of the 1800s, many of these whites paid dearly for their involvement in antiracism, as they faced community ostracism, crossburnings, and death threats. These interracial organizations, along with the Highlander Folk School (founded in 1932 by the black Septima Clark and the white Myles Horton), came under constant attack for their "immoral" race-mixing (Thomas 1996, 54).

The NAACP laid much of the legal groundwork for the civil rights movement of the 1960s, and it is upon this decade that most of the small body of literature on white antiracists focuses. Doug McAdam's *Freedom Summer* (1988) and Alphonso Pinkney's *The Committed* (1968) are two sociological studies of white civil rights activists of the 1960s, both of which make use of anonymous surveys and interviews with these whites. These two scholars are both particularly concerned with the factors that motivated whites to participate in the movement. Both find that religious and/or secular humanist values were important in compelling whites to become activists for civil rights. They felt it was the morally right thing to do. Pinkney (1968) cites these whites' persistence in the face of massive resistance (e.g., being jailed, losing their jobs, being ostracized by friends and family, receiving threats of death and/ or harm) as testament to their commitment to the cause. Pinkney (1968) even names six white "martyrs" of this period, including

Reverend Jonathan Daniels, Reverend James Reeb, and Mrs. Viola Liuzzo. Sara Evans, in her book *Personal Politics* (1980), focuses on the role of southern white women in the movement, among them Anne Braden, Casey Hayden, and Mary King. There is even the problem of whites' role in the civil rights movement of the 1960s being overexaggerated, as films like *Mississippi Burning,* among others, have been criticized for doing. We do not have to look too hard to be reminded of white activism during the 1960s, whether it be civil rights or any other type of activism.

Yet the 1960s are but a faint memory, if that, for much of today's adult population. Contemporary college students might well find the 1960s to be ancient history, hardly a factor even in their own parents' lives. Today, most white Americans get a majority of their information about race relations from TV (Steinhorn and Diggs-Brown 2000), and the images that television projects when the subject of racism is broached are usually of African American leaders like the Reverends Jesse Jackson, Al Sharpton, and Louis Farrakhan. When we see whites taking action around racial issues, it is usually KKK and neo-Nazi groups that are profiled on news magazine and talk show television. Or it is the "angry white man" whose job or slot in college has supposedly been taken from him because of affirmative action. Ignatiev and Garvey (1996) attempt to counteract this cultural silence about contemporary white antiracism by publishing individual accounts of "race traitors." But on the whole, the relative silence about today's white antiracists is the norm. Those who are continuing in this long tradition of white antiracists today are seldom seen or heard.

RESEARCHING WHITE ANTIRACISTS

As the group White Women Challenging Racism (Thompson and White Women Challenging Racism 1997) made clear in the opening pages of this chapter, white antiracists often lack a sense of membership to a larger historical collective. One of their priorities is to avoid "reinventing the wheel"—that is, they long to know what other whites have found effective in challenging racism. Whites need to draw upon this long tradition detailed above, so that they do not have to start from scratch, but it is often not readily available. Moreover, as previously noted, today's forms of racism are often more covert and unacknowledged than slavery or Jim Crow, so whites need more contemporary answers to the question "What can I do?" than their ancestors who fought for abolition and desegregation can give them. I can think of few better ways to demonstrate what whites can do to fight racism than to go to the source—today's white antiracists themselves.

I interviewed thirty North American white antiracists for this study, between 1996 and 1999.[3] The respondents were selected using a purposive snowball sampling technique. My purpose was to gather as wide a variety of white antiracists as possible, in terms of geographic region, age, and socioeconomic status. I also deliberately selected an even number of men and women for the study (fifteen each) because the scant research done previously on white antiracists in the 1990s usually relied solely on women and feminist networks (e.g., Eichstedt 1997; Feagin and Vera 1995; Frankenberg 1993). The methods appendix provides a more detailed profile of each respondent's gender, age, organizational membership, and antiracist activities, as well as a summary of their geographic locations.

There were some aspects of interviewing protocol for white antiracists which are not at all addressed in most traditional methods handbooks. One thing that was particularly important to nearly all of these respondents was knowing about my own identity as an antiracist. Not only did they want to know whether I was antiracist, but they also wanted to know *why* I was, and what had motivated me to be so—some as a condition of being interviewed, others as a condition of being more open and candid during the interview process. Additionally, a statement in the "informed consent" form assuring the respondents that their real name would not be used in my reports, which might ordinarily result in more comfort and candor with the interview, actually left many interviewees disappointed. Given the historical amnesia about white antiracists I have already discussed here, a good number of the respondents felt strongly that their real names *should* be used if at all possible. They expressed the hope that they could connect with other antiracists, build networks, and become known for the work they were proud of doing.[4] In this way, the project departed somewhat from traditional research methods in order to allow for more

comfort for the respondents, but more importantly to form community—between myself and other white antiracists as well as between the respondents and any other antiracists who might read
the book (including other respondents). This was in keeping with
the larger goal of the study: to facilitate visibility and connection
between white antiracists so they would not need to reinvent the
wheel.

Although the interviews make up the bulk of the data used here,
the analysis would not have been complete without the archival
analysis and participant observation I did with antiracist groups
and their members. Half (fifteen) of the respondents belonged to
one of two antiracist organizations—Anti-Racist Action (ARA) or
the People's Institute for Survival and Beyond (PI)—which are described in detail in the next section. As a participant observer, I
joined ARA in protesting a KKK demonstration in Ohio in 1996.
Then, in 1997, I accompanied one ARA organizer to a concert in
which he distributed information about ARA and signed up people on the mailing list to receive *ARA News*, its free biannual publication. As part of that effort, I answered questions and provided
information about the group and offered information about how
they could join. In 1998 one other white person and I coordinated
an ARA chapter in Florida for the duration of one semester, which
included many efforts of recruitment ("tabling") like that which I
participated in at the concert, as well as updating phone lists and
presiding over meetings. I also participated in one of PI's intense
two-and-one-half-day Undoing Racism workshops in 1998.

To get to know these organizations, their missions and practices
as clearly as possible, I also reviewed any written materials they
produced, including brochures, pamphlets, newsletters, and
books. Additionally, I exchanged written correspondence with key
organizers from each group as we dialogued about their philosophies. Even when interviewees did not belong to ARA or PI, they
sometimes provided me with written information about their own
activities in groups, such as New Abolitionists, Race Traitors, and
Institutes for the Healing of Racism. While I do not make these
groups a key part of the analysis here, reading about them helped
me to reach a greater understanding of the diversity of antiracist
experiences and to see more clearly the origins of these particular
individuals' motivations and philosophies. It will become evident

throughout this text that it is impossible to fully comprehend the experiences of white antiracist activists without factoring in the organizations which have inspired and shaped them. In this work I focus on ARA and PI to illuminate this point.

ANTI-RACIST ACTION AND THE PEOPLE'S INSTITUTE FOR SURVIVAL AND BEYOND

Anti-Racist Action (ARA) was officially founded in the early 1990s in the cities of Columbus, Ohio; Minneapolis; and Toronto, mostly by white individuals to counteract Ku Klux Klan and neo-Nazi activity in their communities (see Novick 1997; Franklin 1998). Counterdemonstrations at Klan rallies drew initial memberships, and youths wanting to protest right wing hate groups that were forming at their schools followed suit. Now there are close to a hundred chapters in the United States alone. Although ARA is sometimes criticized for its focus on the racism of these "fringe" groups, the *ARA News* exposes how these groups are not so "fringe" after all. This newsletter, with subscribers in the tens of thousands, also serves to educate about racism (and other forms of hatred) happening around the country through its collage of newspaper clippings and commentaries. Another form of education ARA provides to the community is its visits to local schools to give presentations. ARA focuses predominantly on frontline activism, and its newest and most famous such project is Copwatch—a system of videotaping and police misconduct litigation that "polices the police" in urban neighborhoods (Selena and Katrina 1996). ARA's emphasis on overt forms of racism is evident in the four main principles all of its various chapters abide by:

1. We go where they go. Whenever racists/fascists are organizing or active in public, we confront them and do our best to stop them.
2. We don't rely on the cops or courts to do our work or to protect us.
3. We defend and support each other in spite of our differences.
4. We are active with the goal of building a movement against racism, sexism, anti-Semitism, homophobia and discrimina-

tion against the disabled, the oldest, the youngest and the weakest of our society (from an organizational memo "What to Do: An Introduction to ARA").

Although ARA is a network of many different chapters with different foci and expertise, they all agree to uphold these four principles.

The People's Institute for Survival and Beyond (PI) was originally founded in 1980 in New Orleans by Jim Dunn and Ron Chisom, two African American men, as a training institute for those in social service professions which served primarily communities of color. PI is most noted for its Undoing Racism workshops, which are now offered on a national scale and serve as transformative experiences for whites confronting racism. Perhaps the best way to explain the workshop is to list what it is *not*: "The Undoing Racism workshop is not . . . a quick fix, a sensitivity session, a guilt trip, a sexism/classism workshop, a training in reducing individual acts of prejudice, [or] a lecture" (Chisom and Washington 1997, 88–89). While ARA concentrates on more overt acts of racism, one of PI's workshop topics is "how well-intentioned individuals and institutions unwittingly maintain racist policies, biases, systems and benefits" (Chisom and Washington 1997, 87); this indicates attention to covert and unintentional forms of racism. Focusing on institutionalized racism as a barrier to community organizing, the workshop trainers delve extensively into historical and contemporary race relations and rely on a Malcolm X-like philosophy that whites should be doing separate work in their own communities. As such, PI has a white subsidiary group called European Dissent ("dissenting what has been done in the European name") of which all of the PI respondents here are members. PI also has four principles:

1. That *racism* has historically been the most critical barrier to unity in this country. It continues to be the primary cause of our failure to overcome poverty and bring about justice.
2. That *culture* is the life support system of the community. Organizers must understand and respect indigenous culture and cultural diversity.
3. That *militarism* is applied racism. It is a pervasive cultural,

economic, and political force that undercuts all efforts to
work for justice and peace.

4. That *history* is a guide to the future. We take seriously the
   notion that those who fail to learn from history are condemned to repeat it (from an informational brochure).

These principles indicate that, compared to ARA, PI is dedicated
toward understanding/education as opposed to action. While
ARA also does education and PI also does action, these are not the
primary foci of their principles. Further, a comparison of the two
organizations' principles reveals that ARA sees other "isms" as
just as important, while PI sees them as secondary and racism as
"primary." The organizations also differ in that PI makes explicit
acknowledgment of race differences within their movement while
ARA does not.

Both ARA and PI are antiracist organizations which draw large
proportions of white members. As such, they were an ideal source
for obtaining sizable numbers of white antiracists to interview. At
the beginning of my research, as places to find respondents seemed
to me to be their only relevance to my work. However, once I began
analyzing what those respondents had to say about being antiracist—from what inspired them to become antiracists to what they
did every day—it became evident that what they did and how they
did it had everything to do with the role of ARA or PI in their lives.
How these groups "frame"[5] racism and what we can do about it
will become a recurring influence throughout the text.

WHITE ALTERNATIVES

It was only many years after Malcolm X had told a white woman
there was "nothing" she could do about racism that he decided
there was an alternative answer. Now over thirty years after
Malcolm X's death, that alternative model of whiteness he advocated—of whites working on racism in their own communities—
has yet to make it into the mainstream discourse of race relations.
Fighting the historical amnesia, asserting that there *is* something
whites can do (besides to pat themselves on the back for not being
KKK members) is an important task of this book. In fact, without a

sizeable white antiracist presence (as there was in the era of 1960s civil rights gains) we have little hope of achieving any further change, much less of fighting all the rollbacks of civil rights that are currently taking place. So making visible what white antiracism looks like today is crucial for the nation's future.

Still, there is another layer of misinformation to address and another layer of white alternatives to uncover. Specifically, I will argue that not only is there something for whites to do, there is much more than just one thing for whites to do and more than just one way for them to do it. Because my sample includes men and women, and some members from two very different antiracist organizations, what little we know about white involvement in antiracism will expand a great deal. Answers which were once unanimous will become multidimensional. That activists do not have to fit one basic profile to join in the struggle against white supremacy opens up possibilities for a stronger and broader-based movement.

The multiple possibilities for white antiracism will be explored in several ways in this text. First, chapter 2 takes up a question that scholars of the white antiracists of the 1960s were also interested in—what motivated these whites to commit their lives to fighting white supremacy? Gender and various life experiences play important roles in the different answers to this question. Here I also begin to explore how organizations are important, because their recruitment efforts and/or their workshops often serve as catalysts for that motivation. Chapter 3 moves to the different frames of antiracism, outlining in much more depth how organizations shape what people do to challenge racism. I examine the definitions of racism that PI and ARA use which respectively frame how they do their work. It will become evident in this analysis that all antiracism is not alike. For readers concerned with immediately answering the question "what can I do?" Chapters 4 and 5 will be central. Chapter 4 looks at what we can do about racism on a personal level—challenging racist comments or jokes, individual actions—while chapter 5 presents what we can do about racism on an institutional level—challenging structures of churches, schools, and occupational settings. Rather than how-to instructions, anecdotes from white antiracists of attempts that have both succeeded and failed lead the discussion. How one deals emotionally with such success and failure is discussed in chapter 6, as these whites are certainly

not exempt from the deeply rooted internalization of racial messages, and these then affect their psyche in ways that are unique to
white antiracists (i.e., becoming angry at all whites for their role
in racism and dissociating from them). Organizational affiliation
affects white antiracists' level of awareness about these internal
emotional processes and of how to cope with them. In the final
chapter (chapter 7) I weave together the organizational approaches
addressed throughout the different chapters, and speculate on the
potential for coalition building between these groups. An appendix
includes contact information so that readers can hopefully get involved with antiracist groups in their area, or at least become more
aware of the diversity of antiracist groups who are continuing that
historical tradition, even if out of mainstream sight.

NOTES

1. Anti-Racist Action (ARA) and the People's Institute for Survival and Beyond (PI) are the two central organizations in this study, and they will be
explained in detail later in this chapter.

2. The white antiracists studied here all focus on some aspect of this broad
definition, but not always all of it, since it may be impractical (even undesir-
able) to focus on each and every type of racism simultaneously.

3. I also occasionally draw upon interviews of five black antiracists (who
were asked for their opinions about white antiracists) which were completed
in 2000 by Jason B. Willis.

4. The appendix indicates whether each interviewee has chosen to go by
his or her real name or a pseudonym here.

5. What little research that has been done on white antiracists has analyzed
them independent of any social movement affiliations they had. The concept
of "framing" is an important contribution of social movements researchers
(Snow and Benford 1992; Hunt, Benford and Snow 1994) guiding this aspect
of my work.

2

"I WAS BORN ON RACE STREET"— HOW WHITES BECOME ANTIRACIST

> I was born on Race Street. R-A-C-E! . . . I'd always heard that from my parents, but I never thought about what that meant. And so ever since then, my kids, when anybody says to them, "How long has your mother been doing this?" They say, "She was born on Race Street." So, I just think it's always been with me. I can't think of a time that I didn't—I didn't know what the word racism meant or anything, I'm not saying that—but I can never think of a time when I didn't think that the world was unfairly divided between what happened to people of color and what happened to white people.

Nancy, one of the white antiracists I interviewed, spoke the words above as if there was never a question in her mind that her life would be dedicated to challenging white supremacy. Yet something that seemed like such a given to her is actually quite uncommon for most whites. In fact, Philomena Essed has noted that "dominant group members who take a clear stand against racism, or who otherwise identify with the Black cause, may under certain circumstances become substitute targets of racism" (1991, 43). Not only is it "abnormal" to be white and concerned about racism in an active way, but one quite possibly opens oneself up to serious consequences as a "substitute target" of racist activity. It is both an unpopular and unsafe place to be. Frederick Douglass once said,

"Power concedes nothing without a demand." Why are some whites not only conceding power without a demand, but putting themselves in jeopardy by taking a personal interest in antiracism? What has motivated them to take a step which is unheard of for most whites? Only a minimum of scholars have considered this question.

There are three main possible explanations for how and why whites become antiracist. The first is that whites get involved through *activist networks*. Either they are involved in some other activist group (e.g., political, religious, environmental) or they have friends who are activists who convince them to go along. This idea was advanced by Doug McAdam (1988) via his research on whites who were active in the 1960s civil rights movement. The second line of thought is that whites must develop *empathy* for people of color by way of "approximating experiences." Either they do it by way of analogy to some oppression they have suffered ("overlapping approximations,") by knowing a person of color and being witness to their suffering ("borrowed approximations,") or by relating to their democratic principles ("global approximations.") Research on this idea has been done mainly on white women (Eichstedt 1997; Hogan and Netzer in Feagin 1993; and Vera 1995), so it is unclear whether men are also motivated by empathy. Finally, I am going to consider an explanation which emerged from the testimony of my respondents: that a particular event in someone's life could serve as a "turning point" and they see their antiracist transformation as dating from that moment. I use the term "planting seeds" (which I borrowed from one of my respondents, Lisa) to describe these early memories. Whether activist networks, empathy, or planting seeds was the main factor in a white person's becoming antiracist varied, and had to do with a combination of each individual's environment, social status (especially gender), and life experiences.

ACTIVIST NETWORKS

Doug McAdam (1988) did research on white students' involvement with the "high-risk" activism of Freedom Summer. Focusing on the voter registration drive for Mississippi blacks sponsored by the

Student Nonviolent Coordinating Committee (SNCC) in the summer of 1964, McAdam conducted a large-scale survey and in-depth interview study of the whites who participated in this effort. He selected this particular segment of the civil rights movement because it was the action in which the highest percentage of whites took part. Challenging the notion that these whites were rebellious students or Communist inspired, McAdam found that Communists were a small minority and that most of the white students involved saw themselves as furthering mainstream democratic or religious values that were a part of their upbringing. Most of them were Northern college students from elite, privileged backgrounds and did not stand to reap much material gain from this "high-risk" action. McAdam demonstrated three major factors influencing these whites' participation in Freedom Summer:

1. organizational ties (whether these be political, religious, or social, as in a campus club);
2. prior participation in some kind of activism (90% had done so locally); and
3. personal relationships with others involved in the movement.

Thus, activist networks were important in motivating whites to antiracist action. To a lesser extent, an ideology of democratic or religious notions of equality was a motivational factor for some, but this was usually not without an organizational basis.

Several of my white antiracist respondents had ties to other organizations, had been involved in prior activism, or were a part of a network of other activists as well. When I asked Pierce what motivated him to become an antiracist activist, he responded:

Mm, it's hard to distinguish that from all the other movement causes that I've been a part of. I've been an activist since I was in high school and was trying to oppose the Vietnam war. And there was a racist element to that, from some perspectives, if you want to count that, that would be the first thing. As far as specifics, in America, racism always boils down to black and white issues. I didn't do anything on that that comes to mind right off hand directly until I moved to [his current residence] about ten years ago, and got involved with progressive groups of different kinds, and trying to oppose the extreme right in several different areas. There've been a number of Ku Klux Klan, Nazi and the

like, demonstrations and other activities in the area that I've been a part
of practically since I moved here.

Mac, an ARA member and organizer who is roughly the same age
as Pierce, got his start in activism around the same time with the
Vietnam war issue. Mac stated:

> What made me aware of racism and all that was really not so much that
> particular issue at all. What happened was I became interested in being
> a radical. And then suddenly I wanted to learn about all the issues. You
> know, I wanted to know about women's rights, and what I was that
> was fucked up that I should unlearn, and how I could understand it.

As with the Freedom Summer white students, Mac and Pierce both
saw antiracist activism as a logical extension of their other activism
efforts, which originate with their antiwar protests during the Vietnam era. David, a PI member and organizer, also dates his first
involvement with antiracism from when he became a campus activist during the Vietnam war years. In more recent years, however, the campus activist spirit has also been a motivator for the
midtwenties generation. Kristin reported that "I probably didn't
identify myself as antiracist until probably in college, primarily
because that's when my political awakening really got serious.
And that antiracism would have been brought about by reactions
to racist events that happened on a college campus, that type of
thing." In fact, Kristin vividly recalls one incident when a black
student found a picture of a figure in a noose drawn on his dorm
room door, and the campus responded with an antiracist demonstration. She began to get involved with this and other race-ori-
ented protests, such as when the college attempted to "diversify"
its student body by offering inner city juvenile delinquents free
tuition. Holly, another ARA member and activist of Kristin's generation, also became involved with antiracism through the spirit of
campus activism. Of her first participation in activism, she recalled:

> There was a demonstration on campus that was supposed to be against
> bigotry. And it was right after—it's kind of funny—Larry Kramer of
> ACT UP [radical AIDS awareness action group] came to speak, and he's
> such a moving speaker. He was one of the founders—really aggressive

and very emotional speaker. So all these people came to hear him, and everyone was so mad afterwards, and there was this march against bigotry at the same time, like that night, and all the people who had gone to Larry Kramer just sort of like—not all of them, but some of them—just sort of naturally went into this demo, which was going to the house of the president of the college.

From this point, she began hanging out with more "countercultural white people," and her activist network of friends led her to more awareness of racism, to where she would eventually work with people of color and learn a lot more. Yet all of these stories have in common the fact that they date their first involvement with antiracism work back to activist networks of other whites on related issues.

When there is a preexisting organization in the area to get involved with, friends often persuade others to get involved and before they know it, they have other committed activists. This is the case with ARA members as well as those affiliated with PI. Jason, an ARA member, says he had always had strong values of equality—"I've always held it in my mind that we're all on the same team"—but it was not until the influence of other activist friends that he became involved in ARA. Jason said, "I knew some of the ARA people and they said "we meet every Monday at [location]" and I had a chance to go to meetings and actually start taking an active part, and contribute what talents I had to the effort." Jason contributed his knowledge of computers, and began coordinating the group's Internet access, formatting their newsletters, and participating in any demonstration that came along the way.

Interestingly, even though Joel is no longer a member of ARA, he credits the presence of ARA in his community for his initial awareness about racism, and his eventual conviction that racism was a more important issue than any other type of activism he had done before.

So I bounced around from antinuclear to Central American solidarity to animal rights to Earth First to [I laugh] South Africa antiapartheid. And I was always the youngest person in all the groups, and no one was as radical as I was . . . so basically my politics were just against all forms of oppression as an anarchist. And in Minneapolis there's a really dynamic group of folks my age, called Anti Racist Action. [Me: Right,

I've talked to some members of that group.] Yeah, this was the early
incarnation of ARA, one of the first. At the time, you could count on
about fifty youth at a meeting, and I have yet to see that replicated
actually at a regular town meeting outside from conferences. But, so
anyway there was a really dynamic group and they were doing stuff
and so I jumped in. And of course I was against racism because I was
against all forms of oppression, and they were also against sexism and
homophobia and stuff, so that fit my politics. And they were activism,
and that's what I was looking for most. And only I think after I got in
there and started reading what folks were reading. . . . I began to realize
the centrality of white supremacy to just about every institution in this
country and the important role that black folk have played in particular
in fighting for a more democratic society. And so I figured if I consider
myself a radical who wants a more democratic society, that's where I
should be borrowing from, not the traditional left that's mired in all
that same problems of racism and white chauvinism and stuff like that.
So I kind of fell into it and then realized later on just how important it
was.

Because one of the first ARA chapters happened to be in his hometown, Joel ended up fiercely committed to combating white supremacy in a way he might not have been at all, or at least not until
much later. Having an active antiracist group in town makes it
much more likely that whites will get involved, especially if there
are other whites in the group.

Fortunate enough to be living in the city where PI was founded,
several PI members credited the two-and-one-half-day Undoing
Racism workshop with motivating their start in activism. They
were often invited to the workshop by a friend who had either
already done it or had heard good things about it. Many stories
were similar in that they knew there was "something" wrong in
terms of racism, but did not develop an understanding and commitment about it until the workshop. Lisa had come to work for PI
as an administrative volunteer on behalf of her church and had
done some "social worky" things that made her want to help people, but did not see herself as antiracist until after the workshop.
Rosalind, who is also a member of PI, did the workshop with her
church and started doing antiracist work at her job and community
from that point on. Additionally, she convinced her husband,
Henry, to take part in the workshop, and has been working on her

grown son and his girlfriend as well. Another PI member, Pam, also talked about friends' recruiting her to the workshop:

> Some friends of mine started making me even more aware of things I'd always known but kind of, I guess, never really put in the forefront or took real notice of, and then some other people that you've probably already spoken with that are friends of mine, who got a friend involved, who got a friend—who got me involved, in the workshop, and that was just amazing.

Since then Pam has not only been vigilant about transforming the racist atmosphere in the school where she teaches, but has attended every single workshop that PI has offered in her hometown since then. In fact, everyone I interviewed who had been to a workshop tried at least once to convince me to attend one also. Thus, when activist networks are available and present to whites, they often get involved the way that McAdam describes: through the influence of other activist friends, other types of activism, and other organizational memberships, such as church.

EMPATHY (APPROXIMATING EXPERIENCES)

But activists and their organizations are not always around. Even if they are present in your community, you may not know about them, or know anyone who is involved with them. Still, there is the possibility of becoming antiracist. Some research has suggested that whites can have experiences which help them to form empathy for people of color. Whites who form close relationships with people of color and witness the brutality they face might feel compelled to act after witnessing such atrocities, to which most whites are oblivious. Several of Frankenberg's antiracist white (female) respondents had been romantically involved with people of color and/or had children of color and credited these experiences as major motivators to speak out on the injustices of racism, even in the absence of familial or social support from other whites. In fact, it was sometimes the negative reaction of whites who were close to them that propelled them to action. Herbert Aptheker, in his historical review of the first two hundred years of antiracism in the

United States (1992), also found that having had "significant experiences with people of African origin" (xiv) was a frequently occurring characteristic among white antiracists. Given the highly segregated nature of U.S. society, particularly in the case of African Americans who are "hypersegregated" more than any other group (Massey and Denton 1992), such experiences were and are fairly rare for most whites.

Aptheker also found lower class whites and women to be highly represented among antiracists. Indeed, in the rare instances when race relations scholars have considered what motivates whites to become antiracists, the focus is usually exclusively on women (Frankenberg 1993; Hogan and Netzer 1993 cited in Feagin and Vera 1995). Focusing on the concept of empathy with people of color as a necessary prerequisite for white antiracism, Feagin and Vera (1995) have suggested that women's experiences with sexism might situate them as more likely to be able to empathize with the racism that people of color face. They argue that whites who have had "some personal experience with exploitation, discrimination or oppression are more likely than other whites to understand the situation of and empathize with African-Americans" (1995, 175). This might explain why members of the lower class, having experienced classism, and women, having experienced sexism, were frequently cited in Aptheker's historical review. However, some preliminary unpublished work by Hogan and Netzer (1993, cited in Feagin and Vera 1995), has found that multiple socially stigmatized statuses were more likely to motivate empathy and antiracism for women than simply the status of being female. For example, Jewish and/or lesbian women were "better able than other white women to empathize with the discrimination faced by African Americans" (1995, 176). Eichstedt's (1997) research on white antiracists also found additional experiences of oppression to be common for white antiracist women. Not only were being Jewish and lesbian important sources of empathy for her respondents, but many also saw their experiences as targets of incest or sexual abuse as another form of "abuse of power" that enabled them to better empathize with victims of racist oppression.

Summarizing these different routes to empathy as motivators for white antiracist action, Hogan and Netzer developed three types of "approximating experiences" that characterized the white antiracist women whom they interviewed. Some used ''borrowed approximations,'' which means that they learned about racism through stories told to them by people of color, whether they were friends or intimate partners, that made racism become real in their minds as a problem needing to be addressed. This is where some of Frankenberg's respondents who had families of color and those antiracists whom Aptheker described as having significant experiences with blacks would fit in. Others used "global approximations," in the absence of any substantial ties to people of color, to relate to racism by seeing it as an unfair crime against humanity, a wrong that needs to be righted to further the cause of justice. In this case a firm belief in wanting to do the right thing could become a source of empathy and a motivator of activism. The third category these scholars proposed is "overlapping approximations," whereby whites empathize with the pain of racism by relating their own analogous experiences of oppression—these could be women, "lower class" whites, gay/lesbian/bisexual/transgender (GLBT) whites, Jewish whites, or even those who had experienced sexual abuse as in Eichstedt's research.

Borrowed Approximations

"Borrowed approximations" were the most common in my research. For Scott, he said his first antiracist action began in "sixth or seventh grade" when he befriended the only black boy in his school, who was often the target of insults and attacks, so much that he ended up transferring to a different school. Scott said:

> My first activistic stance was that a couple of ignorant yahoos had him [his black friend] cornered during recess one day, trying to shake him down for his lunch money. I guess my first act was actually pretty physical [laughs] because I knocked a couple heads together and actually threw the other one into the ground and told him to "Get the hell out! What's your problem?!" [and they responded with] that kind of reaction, "Why don't you stick to your own kind?!" . . . and that's when I realized that I was surrounded by a bunch of idiots, a bunch of closed-minded fools [laughs].

This action cost Scott much social disapproval and eventually ended what might have been quite a successful football career be-

cause of the ostracism of his peers. In college he later did participate in political demonstrations, and in graduate school acted as
an ally to a group of students of color's demands after racist incidents, but rather than being a part of an activist network, he has
done his work on more of an individual basis, including the racism
he confronts on a daily basis defending his Mexican wife and children.

Also witnessing the "why don't you stick to your own kind"
white mentality, Travis was converted to the antiracist cause
through "borrowed approximations"—seeing not only the racism
that people of color in his life faced, but also the reaction other
whites received when associating with them.

> A black family and then an East Indian family moved into the neighbor-
> hood and I got to see how the neighbors actually treated them, and it
> was pretty bad. They were beaten and eggs thrown at them, and for no
> reason that I could see, they were harassed constantly—the kids beaten
> up by other kids, the adults shunned by the other adults. And my
> mother had started dating a black man at this point, and for that I was
> shunned and beaten by other kids just because of the race mixing, as
> they called it. . . . My actions basically took the form of—when I was
> twenty I started dating somebody of color and people would see, and
> call this person who's Asian a gook or something, and I took offense to
> it and usually retaliated to it.

Like Scott, Travis began his antiracist activism without the support
of a larger activist community, but was compelled by the racism
he witnessed due to people of color in his life. When a local ARA
chapter became active in his hometown, he was right there to join
in, but this action was an extension of a position he had already
taken in his life, and he does not credit ARA with giving him his
start. Rather, his borrowed approximations from earlier experiences are what he credits for making him antiracist.

Borrowed approximations can also come from the testimony of
people of color who are not even friends or acquaintances. In Olivia's case, she credits written word (literature by people of color)
and spoken word (rap music by African Americans) for her awareness of what it is like to face racism, which led her to become active
about it. Like Travis, she later joined an ARA in her community.
Similarly, Mike credits sociology readings for his antiracist impe-

tus. In particular, he mentions Jonathan Kozol's *Savage Inequalities*, which chronicles the educational racism which Mike later experienced firsthand teaching elementary school in the inner city. Given his outrage about these conditions, taking the PI workshop only gave him confirmation of what he already knew, but gave him the organizational backing to do something more about it. He is now involved with the People's Youth Agenda, which reaches out to young people with antiracist educational activities like Freedom School. While Hogan and Netzer's concept of borrowed approximations referred to personal acquaintances with people of color, this research reveals that borrowed approximations can also be obtained through literature, music, and other forms of expression in which people of color portray their experiences with racism. This is an important point, given the extreme racial segregation in our society: even when whites are not personally acquainted with people of color, there are still chances for borrowed approximations to occur.

Overlapping Approximations

Not unlike those respondents who had experienced interracial friendships and/or relationships, Amy dated her first awareness of racism back to dating a black boy in high school. She learned about racism through stories that he told her, and began to especially "take things personally" when she became pregnant with his baby, envisioning herself as a future mother of a black child. She said, "Racism was the first 'ism' I became aware of, and then once I became aware of that, everything just followed really easily. I started calling myself a socialist and all of these other things. I attributed that to being antiracist, I thought I was. Now I would say that I wasn't." Although "borrowed approximations" began her awareness, Amy stated that it was not until she relied upon "overlapping approximations," relating her own oppression to that of people of color, that she would call herself antiracist. This happened when she came out as a lesbian during her college years. She said at that point her understanding of racism changed from being a personal issue to an institutional one (see chapter 3 for more on this ideological shift). Additionally, it was by understanding her own oppression as a woman and as a lesbian that she began to empathize with the goals of separatism. Previously she had rejected separatist ideology because it meant that some of the closest people in her life, who were African American, would no longer be there for her if they chose to separate from white people. But it was by understanding her own oppression that she understood institutional structures of oppression and began to support the idea of occasional voluntary separation of oppressed groups.

Two female ARA members also drew analogies between their own oppression and that of people of color under the system of racism. Using this overlapping approximation, Ani said her outrage at bigotry comes firsthand, from being Jewish. Ani later got involved with ARA but already carried with her an antiracist position. Olivia, who used borrowed approximations from literature and music, also credited overlapping approximations for part of her activism: "I could never experience the pain . . . that an African American person [does] . . . the closest I've ever come to that is that I'm bisexual myself and I've gotten a lot of intimidation from people like that [which people of color face] and I've had a lot of pain." Like Amy, being a member of a sexual minority allowed Olivia to develop empathy with the discrimination that people of color face by relating it to her own "pain."

Supporting Eichstedt's research, Nancy recounted how her early experiences with physical and sexual abuse predicated her antiracism:

> My father was a physically abusive person, and he was also sexually abusive . . . if you'd told me the word oppression as a kid, I would not have known what in the world that meant . . . but as an adult I think that there are a lot of things that seem similar to me between being abused and seeing others abused. There was a feeling that people picked out someone—maybe in a family or somewhere outside the family—and ascribed all kinds of terrible things to that person, and then it was OK to do whatever you did. . . . And it just seemed very similar to me to what happened to the African American people around me.

Although she said she did not have terms like "oppression" and "stigmatize" in her vocabulary at the time, she already understood that individuals could abuse their power over others for no good reason, and then turn around and blame it all on them. Nancy also credits this form of empathy for her conviction that people of color did not need to be "taken care of" or treated as "victims."

For this sample of both male and female white antiracists, it is evident that *overlapping approximations are used exclusively by women*. This is interesting, because women are not the only ones who can be oppressed along nonracial lines. Men can also be gay, Jewish, or located at the bottom of the class structure, and any of these could be the impetus for overlapping approximations. However, it seems that at least for this sample, white men doing antiracist work were not as much motivated by any oppression that they had faced themselves as were white women.

Global Approximations

Global approximations, where antiracists rely on general humanitarian ideas of fairness and equality to motivate them, were difficult to find in isolation. These sentiments were spoken by many of the respondents, but they usually became activated when the person witnessed something, read about something, or got involved with an activist network or organization. For example, both Olivia and Jason said they had been raised to "treat everyone the same," but it was not until Olivia started doing some reading, and Jason attended ARA meetings, that they really saw antiracism as something meaningful enough for them to take action. McAdam's work on Freedom Summer also found this to be true. Those who relied upon democratic principles to explain their activism also referred to an organization they belonged to which supported and enhanced these principles. Similarly, global approximations do not appear to be strong enough on their own to motivate antiracist activism for the whites interviewed here.

"PLANTING THE SEED"—NARRATIVE LINKAGES

Although activist networks seem to be a factor when activists are already around, and borrowed approximations or overlapping approximations (for women) also are influential, there are certain commonalities among these activists' stories of becoming antiracist that neither of these frameworks have addressed. In my analysis of these data, I became mindful of what Gubrium and Holstein (1997) call narrative linkages. What this means is that even if a respondent mentioned activist friends or a black lover, I did not assume that this was the motivator for their becoming antiracist. Rather, these personal facts only became relevant if the activists themselves linked them to their stories of what was important in making them antiracist.

Polletta's (1998) research on sit-in activists from the 1960s civil rights movement shows that narrative analysis can yield very different results in interpreting movements. Although the civil rights movement had been characterized as orderly and carefully calculated, for those participating, "their narrative construction as spontaneous was central to an emerging collective identity" (Polletta 1998, 153). Thus, even though the sit-ins were very much planned, the activists' narrative linkages were ones of "spontaneity," of energetic breaks with movement elders. In finding out what sparked white antiracists to action, then, it is important to pay attention to narrative linkages, and how the respondents construct their antiracist "births."

When several white antiracists told the stories of their progression into antiracist consciousness and activism, they vividly recalled an early childhood experience that predated their antiracist work but seemed to make them destined to become antiracist eventually. I borrow from Lisa, one of my respondents, the term "planting the seed" to describe this event. When she talked about the frustration of confronting someone's racist practices yet not being able to immediately educate that person successfully, she referred to "that idea of planting the seed, you have no idea what will blossom." She may not convert the person to antiracism right then, but that experience of having made that person think, if only just for a minute, will stay with them and perhaps "blossom" into awareness and/or action at a later date. For some white antiracists, a seed was also planted in their lives, and they referred back to it when talking about what led them to becoming antiracists.

Seeds Planted in School

Mark, who now edits an antiracist journal and is trying to build a movement of "new abolitionists," recalled the moment at which the seed was planted for his antiracist career:

> When I was a junior in high school, which was in 1963, about, in that September, it was four young girls who died in a bombing of a church in Birmingham, Alabama. And the man who I had as an English teacher that year, who was himself just out of college—I was going to a Catholic high school here in [city name] and he came to the class, either the first day—I don't know, it seemed to me it was the first day, thinking back thirty-odd years, and he said, "Let's say a prayer for those four little girls." And no one had ever said anything like that in that school. The school was probably, I think, all white students. And it really affected me. Now I honestly can't tell you what my initial reaction was, whether it was positive or negative, that I don't remember. All that I remember was sort of the scene. And by the time that I left high school two years later, I had developed a friendship with that teacher and had written an essay in the high school literary magazine which was a review of James Baldwin's *The Fire Next Time*, which had just recently been published. . . . But in a sense, my kind of political career around issues of race dates from that moment.

Mark dated his antiracist "birth" back to an experience of a teacher daring to mention an incident of racism in an empathetic manner in the early 1960s. Although he did not even remember his initial reaction to this occurrence, he was certain that it is the moment with which an antiracist potential had begun. This was an epiphany for him, or a turning point at which he made key realizations that continued to have an effect on how he interpreted future events (Denzin 1989). Similarly, referring back to roughly the same time period, PI member David also reminisced about a daring schoolteacher:

> For years I was kind of—inside my own mind and heart I guess you could say—beginning to evolve into a southerner who would break ranks with that which was expected of me. And I was very typical of everyone that I knew. Knew nobody else, *no one*. Knew *no moderates* on

the race issue. There were just degrees of extremism, *nobody*, not *one* person—except in retrospect, a schoolteacher, Vera Miller, when I was a senior in high school, who would come in and write "hate." I remember one time she wrote "hate" on the board and she told us to write, and to not ask any questions. She would put her long fingernails on the top of my head and say "think!" She was seeing something in some of us, and she was trying very carefully, 'cause she'd get fired in a second. She was trying very carefully to try to open up some vistas for us that simply were not going to be allowed anywhere else. I was very impacted by her in retrospect. I look back and begin to see things.

In a southern atmosphere in which even a moderate pondering on the topic of race was grounds for termination of a teacher, David was struck by the bravery of his teacher who cleverly devised ways to bring alternative perspectives into the minds of those she thought had potential. Here a seed was planted for David "to begin to see things," even within his repressive environment.

Antiracists from later generations also referred to seed-planting moments in which they were placed head-to-head against the status quo of racism. Kristin, who later became a campus activist, remembered how it troubled her to see the only black boy in her elementary school face racism in first grade:

I became aware of the fact that when mothers would drop off their beaming white children, they would glance over at him, and I could just see, I started to notice looks being shot to him and that kind of thing and I, for the longest time, my first grade year, spent trying to figure out why everyone looked at him funny and . . . first grade was also the year that I was watching *3-2-1 Contact*. . . . And on that show, during first grade, he [black actor] did a thing about race, and I was watching it, and he was telling me, "the only difference is that, you know, that pigments in the skin and that kind of thing" and I remember sitting there being like, "no way!! That's the only difference?!" [laughs] And like calling my mom and being like, "Mom! Did you know that that's the only difference between me and Greg is that he just has different pigment in his skin?" And I thought I had solved an answer to the world, like, if everyone only knew that, if everyone else was aware of this great amount of knowledge, [laughs] then there would be no problem, and the mothers of the kids in my class wouldn't look at this kid funny, and I wouldn't have to wonder what would happen to me if I sat down on this chair right after him or something. . . . But anyway, so

I called my mom and told her about this and she was kinda like "yeah, you're right!" [laughs] "Uh-huh." And I told her that we should tell everybody, because that would really solve a lot of problems. [laughs] But anyway, so that was my big awakening year.

Although Kristin was only in first grade when this happened, and the black boy (whose first and last name she vividly remembered) and his family moved out of the white-majority suburb shortly thereafter, this was a crucial point in Kristin's memory of how race became a part of her life. Like for Mark and David, Kristin's anti-racist activism did not begin until later when she became a "campus activist," yet this event stayed alive in her consciousness of how she grew into a person who would break from the norm of how whites regard race.

Seeds of Desire for Difference

Other whites described seed-planting experiences that seemed to come from nowhere specific. They only knew that they wanted to be around people of color. Once they had been around people of color, they began to develop the borrowed approximating experiences that Hogan and Netzer describe. Yet the fact that they, unlike most whites, wanted to hang around people unlike themselves racially, was an interesting similarity shared by several of the respondents—the seeds from which the borrowed approximations began to blossom. Although they often looked back with embarrassment to these moments of naiveté or cultural appropriation, they did relate them as the stepping stones toward eventual awareness. Susan wanted to be around people who were culturally different from herself, and even though she did not exactly know why she wanted to do so, this desire in itself was a seed that would eventually blossom:

I had ended up applying for an assistantship that supposedly was open in the Office of Multicultural Affairs, and I look back on my application now, and to me, multicultural affairs was sort of like international students—that's how little informed I was [laughs] . . . and when I read their description, I realized it's something very different than international student affairs, but I considered myself a liberal . . . and knowing what they were doing, I believed in it, just from what I'd read about what they were up to. So I went in and went for my internship interview, and [laughs] the question that the director asked me was "Why are you here?" [I said:] "I don't know," you know? It was like, that was the beginning. And, I don't think they'd had a white intern before. . . . And so basically I worked that semester there and I started out thinking I was gonna do stuff like interviewing people of color about their interest in international study abroad and stuff like that. And just realized after the first two weeks that this is not what this is about. And I basically did an entire semester on white awareness. Learning a lot about what it meant to be white. And witnessing a lot of things that students of color were going through, just by talking to people and being around the office a lot.

Being among the students of color, Susan developed what she would eventually call her antiracist stance, in part because of these "borrowed approximations" gleaned from their stories about experiences with racism on campus. Yet she would never have started on that journey without the seed of desire to be around people culturally different from herself. She laughed about that desire when telling her story, because she knew her desire was not rooted in an understanding of racism itself, which she has today. ARA member Holly had a remarkably similar story of wanting to be in a multicultural environment (a dormitory) while in college, even though she was not yet an antiracist. Unlike Susan, however, Holly's naiveté was not given the benefit of the doubt and she did not get the position:

I was interested in living in the Third World house. Just, I don't know why, and I applied, and there was like this interview process and everything, and I flunked it completely. [Me: You did?] Yeah, yeah! Like [laughs] they asked me, "Ok, what's the definition of the Third World?" I passed that question fine; I said, "well, any place that's been colonized and screwed around by Europe." And I felt pretty good about myself then. I had the right answer. And then they asked, "Well what's your experience in dealing with people of color and what did you learn that you would apply to find better relationships?" . . . [laughs, then replies:] "Well, I come from [city name]; it's like a multicultural city, you know, I don't think I really have any problem." [laughs] I could just see the way they're looking, some guy was like, "Oh, God, I don't know." [laughs] But they sent me this nice letter, that said, "We don't think this is a really good place for you, but keep thinking about your issues and educating yourself." And I just felt like a complete loser. [laughs] [Me: That's interesting.] Mm-hm [pause] I mean, I knew they were totally right because I had like totally unexamined things, like I would have been a pain in the ass for people who are trying to learn about themselves and be assertive about their identity. I just would have been the person they had to argue with, or who'd be constantly sucking up and making them pissed off or whatever. [laughs]

Like Susan, Holly did not see herself as having an awareness of racism when she applied for the Third World house (and neither did the interviewer, apparently). Yet the seeds of an unexplained desire were there, to be in a position which she said very few white people at the school were actually interested in pursuing. And Holly continued to think about her issues and educate herself, as she was asked, and years later launched her start into antiracist action.

Elizabeth's seed was planted much earlier. She reported an adolescence filled with wanting to be around people of color, particularly men. Her first memory of an encounter with a person of color was when she was ten years old. Her family had befriended a Mexican man from their church, in whom she personally took an interest: "I got to be really good friends with him. In fact, I think I had kind of a crush on him." She recalled, "That was another early memory of just having a real strong attraction—not a sexual one at that age obviously—but some sort of real fascination with difference." This fascination continued into her teen years:

> The first African American person I even knew at all was this one female in my high school and I went to a private Christian school that was real conservative and real white [laughs] and when I was like sixteen or so, I guess, she came to our school. And it was kind of weird, actually in looking back I wonder if there was a curiosity there because I really went after, pursued a friendship with her real hard. I really wanted to be friends with her. And it wasn't like this thing of, "she needs friends so I wanna be her friend," 'cause she had plenty of friends and stuff. It was just, I thought I want to know this person, I want to know what she's like.

Elizabeth said this friend never spoke about racism, so she did not begin to learn about racism until a later friendship with an African

American young man. For her later antiracist position, she credited borrowed approximations from these relationships she continued to pursue, and later overlapping approximations from becoming a feminist and learning about her own oppression as a woman. Elizabeth expressed quite a bit of embarrassment, not unlike Susan and Holly, that her early "fascination" was not motivated by antiracism. In fact, she even called it selfish "co-opting" of someone else's culture. Yet Elizabeth's seemingly unexplained drive to surround herself with difference served as an important springboard into her eventual antiracist activism.

Nancy, whose words form the title of this chapter, cannot remember a time when she did not adore people of color, beginning with a black maid ("Tilly") that her family owned.[1] Although Tilly was grossly mistreated by whites and as a result quite bitter, that did not change Nancy's yearning to be around her. It was a special treat when Tilly would take her to the black church: "I get goose bumps all over remembering, because I loved the experience." In fact, Nancy tells the story of herself as a person for whom, from the moment of her birth, race would always be an issue, as if it were spiritually predetermined, when she recalled being born on Race Street.

Whether it was an unusual preoccupation with people racially different from themselves, or another antiracist voice planting the seeds of dissension in a young child, many white antiracists shared in common the narrative strategy of reaching back before their antiracist activism to find their motivational story. What is striking is how similar some stories are between respondents who do not even know or live near each other. Elementary and middle school students whose teachers left strong impressions on them by breaking the silence and eager liberal college students without a clue about racism mutually held an early experience which they felt was a crucial beginning to their antiracist lives. Although the data here provide evidence for McAdam's theory of activist networks as well as for Hogan and Netzer's approximating experiences framework, it is equally important to pay attention to additional connections that the respondents themselves have made about what has made them antiracist. This finding should also be especially inspiring to white antiracists themselves, who are in the often unrewarding business of planting seeds of their own for others. It is heartening to know that our seeds may someday blossom for someone else years down the road.

HOW CAN WE GET *MORE* WHITES INVOLVED?

Frankenberg (1993) has written: "Many people have chance en-counters with antiracist discourses; the difficult question to answer is why some individuals respond positively to them, while others do not" (159). While this is indeed a question that is difficult to answer with certainty, this research gets us a little closer to some possible answers. First, those who have already done some activ-ism on other "leftist" issues with other whites (e.g., antiwar, envi-ronmentalism) could be more receptive to an antiracist agenda. This finding speaks to the importance of coalitional politics among leftist groups. The "radical right" seems to be able to combine its efforts on several different issues simultaneously. For example, the Christian Coalition can marshal its members' efforts to attack sev-eral different types of policies, including gay rights, reproductive freedom for women, restrictions on pornography, and affirmative action—all from one organization. In contrast, the gay community is not united on the issue of reproductive choice, environmentalists are not united on the issue of affirmative action, and so on, making it less likely that these groups work together and have a chance to get to know their respective ideologies. Yet recent efforts have been made to bridge these gaps. The April 1999 Millions for Mumia march, which was clearly an antiracist action, brought together a variety of activist communities. Mumia Abu-Jamal is an African American man on death row in Philadelphia for allegedly murder-ing a white police officer, even though it was later revealed that "eyewitness" testimony was falsely coerced out of witnesses by police. Seen as a political prisoner because of his affiliation with the Black Panthers, Mumia's case has received global attention and outcry. What was notable about this latest march for his freedom was the diversity of activists in attendance. Groups from Christians opposing the death penalty to Rainbows for Mumia (Gay, Lesbian, Bisexual, Transgender, and Two-Spirit People in support of Mumia) were a part of the event. People who were already activists on issues of injustice and police brutality came to learn how institutional racism was at the core of their concerns, if they did not know already. If more efforts like these are made, my research shows, whites might be more likely to make the connections between antiracism and other activist concerns they already have.

Another reason whites might be more likely to become antiracist is if they somehow witness the oppression of people of color in their lives. Some researchers have already mentioned these "borrowed approximations"—in which whites' empathy is evoked through close contact with people of color—and several of my respondents claim that this was their experience as well. In my own experience, I firmly believe that I may never have known the extent of contemporary racism in the United States if I had not made what was originally a very private and personal decision to date an African American young man. It is part of the white experience that we are "carefully taught" (in PI member David's words) to remain oblivious to racism in our daily lives. Knowing how rare it is that whites have truly intimate relationships with people of color, especially African Americans, it may leave one fairly pessimistic about the possibility of ever having a substantial number of white American antiracists. However, my research suggests that missing from the concept of borrowed approximations is the recognition that this information can come not only from personal relationships but from secondhand sources of creative expression of people of color like literature and music.[2] This study highlighted the importance of such sources in whites' development of an antiracist consciousness.

This finding is particularly important for educators in predominantly white environments, since it suggests that even in the absence of interracial contacts whites can develop some antiracist inspiration through written and spoken word about racism. Knowing this heightens the urgency for material on race and racism to be infused at every level of school curriculum. Upon my own arrival at college, which is not atypical, I found that the general education requirements included a course on women's experience, but not on African Americans, Native Americans, or any other historically oppressed "racial" group. Since white students do not often seek this information voluntarily, it seems imperative that curriculum revision efforts be intensified along these lines, not just in higher education, but at much earlier points in the educational process.

Another empathic experience for whites that has sometimes led them to become antiracist is when they begin to draw connections between oppression they face in their own lives and that which is faced by people of color in our racist society. Prior research has called this an "overlapping approximation." In my study it was only white women who drew upon this approximation, and they did it in a variety of ways. Some linked it to awareness of women's oppression, while others linked it to oppression-based sexual orientation (being bisexual or lesbian), and even being oppressed by sexual abuse and incest was a source of empathy. What is interesting is that, although the previous studies only were done on white women, borrowed approximations in this study were used by men and women alike, and it was only overlapping approximations that seemed gender specific. Because I do not have a random sample of all white antiracists, it is impossible for me to speculate with certainty whether this means women are more prone to be antiracist in general. Even though Aptheker (1992) asserted that historically women were more likely than men to be antiracist, it is my initial impression from my research experiences that whites of both genders are involved in a variety of ways in antiracist activism. In fact, it is not unlikely that sexism may continue to play out in antiracist organizations as it has historically, with men being in more powerful positions in the groups. (Recall that the key organizers I corresponded with in both organizations studied here were men.) But the tendency for white women to relate to antiracism in a way that just as many men do not remains an interesting gender difference worth considering.

There is some research by feminist scholar Carol Gilligan (1982) that suggests that women are more likely to develop a sense of justice by relating personally to things (ethic of care) while men are more likely to draw upon more abstract democratic ideals of fairness (ethic of justice). Additionally, Platt and Fraser's analysis (1998) of letters written to Martin Luther King, Jr., during the 1960s civil rights movement noted a similar difference in how white men and women expressed solidarity with the movement. The women "express[ed] networking with the movement by way of personal ties and men by way of external and institutional ties" (172). However, these authors dismiss the gender difference as a relic of the particular historical period, and Gilligan's research on gender differences has been widely criticized both methodologically and substantively for its assertions (see Greeno and Maccoby 1986). Further, if Gilligan were correct, we might expect the white antiracist men here to use global approximations (objecting to racism on basic principles of equity) to the extent that the women use overlapping approximations. Yet this is not the case. Global approximations were rarely motivational factors for either women or men in this sample. So it is difficult to reach with certainty a reason for this gender difference, which is the only one that emerges in this entire work. We need more studies of men doing other antioppression work, such as feminism or gay rights, which continue to probe the issue of how they develop empathy with an oppressed group when they are not a member of it. Without clear reasons for this difference though, we can still act upon it. Namely, women's groups advocating feminism and lesbian/bisexual rights and providing for survivors of sexual abuse can use analogies to the experiences of people of color in their work to increase white women's involvement in antiracism.

Beyond the existing framework for explaining how whites get involved in antiracism, white antiracists made their own connections about their motivations for action. Relating back to epiphanic moments, several respondents recalled vivid memories which they believe planted the seed of antiracism for their lives. These experiences came before their approximations and/or activist networks, but they refer to them as if they created a necessary predisposition for antiracism. In other words, if these seeds had not been planted, perhaps the respondents may not have encountered their subsequent motivational experience; it might have taken much longer, or the seed was their first motivational experience in and of itself. Some of these seeds consisted of a person who challenged them in their youth to question the existing racial hierarchy, or a strange desire within themselves to break the taboo against interracial socializing without even fully understanding the reason why. Since, as Feagin and Vera (1995) argue, we are trained *not* to empathize with people unlike ourselves, these moments of epiphany were important in whites beginning to develop the empathy needed to start them on their antiracist paths. Once whites are presented with alternative ways of thinking about race that differ from those of the white mainstream, the seed is activated and the journey of growth begins.

It is notable that many of these "seeds" occurred in an educational setting. Yet this is in no way meant to exaggerate the antiracist potential of education. The same educational system that planted seeds in several of these respondents is the same one that teaches racism to many more white children and adults than are represented here. And even highly educated individuals are hardly absent from the most blatant displays of white supremacy we have seen in recent years. In 1996, chief executive officers of the Texaco corporation were implicated in making racial slurs in a business meeting. Even more recently, Matt Hale completed his graduate education in law while spearheading the World Church of the Creator, whose ideology inspired Benjamin Smith in his killing spree targeting blacks, Koreans, and Jews in 1999. On national TV Hale proclaimed that his so-called Church believes we should not feel sorry for the victims of Smith's deadly racist rampage. If any seeds were planted during Hale's education, clearly they have not yet blossomed. We cannot sit back and trust that "education" will cure what is ailing us as a nation.

More specifically, we must aggressively fight for *antiracist* curriculum changes, ones that incorporate the perspectives of people of color from the earliest of ages, and testify to the *current* oppressive conditions in our society. Traditional multicultural approaches which take the "add-diversity-and-stir" approach—singing songs and eating foods from different cultures—do nothing to enlighten students about oppression, both past and present. Amanda Lewis has contrasted traditional multiculturalism with critical multiculturalism or antiracist education. While the former takes the add-and-stir approach to the curriculum, the latter focuses on both content and process (the explicit and the "hidden" curriculum). As Lewis notes:

> Anti-racist education differently locates the origins of student failure. While multicultural education says the system is partly to blame, most of the focus remains on home and culture. On the other hand, antiracist or critical multicultural education says that though you can not [sic] ignore social, cultural and home factors, much of the blame must

be located in institutionalized racism in classroom and school. (Lewis 1999, 27)

Thus, not only does antiracist education change the *content* of the curriculum by adding materials about people of color, it also revamps the hidden curriculum by restructuring the *process* by which racist attitudes are subtly communicated in school. An antiracist education also does not romanticize oppression as a thing of the past, but makes connections on how historical conditions are inextricably tied to the present. In the data presented here, no one's seed was planted by learning about slavery or Martin Luther King, Jr. Teachers who asked students to reflect upon the racial issues of the day or college campus groups that dealt with issues of everyday inequality are the ones that were remembered here. So it is not just education, but a very specific kind of education that needs to be implemented in order to give rise to more of the activist networks, approximating experiences, and planted seeds that inspired the dedicated white antiracists interviewed here.

NOTES

1. Indeed, "owned" is the best word here, since Tilly was given as a "gift" to the family, and there were no wages paid to her.
2. Whites' enjoyment of these forms of cultural expression can often come from a place of appropriation or rebellion, rather than true empathy, so mere exposure should not be considered a sufficient basis for empathy.

3

FRAMING WHITE ANTIRACISMS

> Racism is a sensitive word. . . . It is a Rorschach word, a linguistic
> inkblot test. How you define it reveals something important about
> you, how you see the world, and your place in it.
> —Page, *Showing My Color*

As we have seen, many white antiracists would not have gotten involved in this type of activism if an antiracist organization were not in existence in their communities. Organizations serve as an important resource for educating the public about the continuing existence of racism in their immediate surroundings and encouraging people to get active in doing something about it. Yet we know these organizations are not located in every city, and only about half of the respondents interviewed for this book were even members of such groups. Even so, the significance of these organizations is striking in terms of how they shape antiracists' definitions of racism and thus how they go about doing their antiracist work. From the most personal to the most public decisions, a recurring theme of this book will be how white antiracists rely upon organizational ideology to guide their thought and actions. The difference between the two primary organizations studied here (ARA and PI) is a key factor behind the diversity of white antiracist practices I have stressed.

The concept of "framing," which comes from the study of social movements, is useful in interpreting the impact of these organizations on white antiracists. Snow et al. (Hunt, Benford, and Snow 1994; Snow and Benford 1992) argue that effective movements use both diagnostic and motivational framing to direct members' understanding of a social problem and why it needs to be addressed. They also frame both the antagonist (the "enemy") and the protagonist (the "hero"). For example, the social movement organization called "Truth," which has been organizing antismoking advertisement campaigns, has diagnosed the problem: a culture which condones and glamorizes smoking. As motivators for creating cultural and behavioral change, the staggering figures on tobacco-related deaths are used in the ads. Thus, the movement has both diagnostic and motivational frames. Further, movement members have framed the antagonist as the tobacco industry. Several of their advertisements demonize tobacco company executives as devious plotters out to make a buck who are eager to recruit more smokers with little regard for their eventual deadly fate. What is important to note about the framing of the antagonist is that it was deliberately chosen and not given. Alternatively, they (or another antismoking organization) could have framed consumers of cigarettes as the antagonist and painted them as capitalist materialists with little regard for who they kill with second-hand smoke. Instead, however, smokers have been framed as innocent victims of the antagonist—the tobacco industry. The concept of framing illustrates that ideology is powerful, and it shapes the direction of a movement. Truth's commercials would be very different with an alternative frame.

As such, when antiracist organizations have different frames of *racism*, the social problem which they are addressing, it is no accident that that particular organization's frame affects their discourse on race. Because previous investigations of white antiracists have been limited in scope and number, no organizational variation has been present, and findings about their ideology have been fairly uniform. However, the diversity of white antiracists represented in this particular study allows a closer look at two different organizational frames of antiracism—the one used by PI and the one used by ARA. Although this particular chapter focuses on how their ideologies are framed, in the subsequent chapters it will become evident that white antiracists' day-to-day activities are often shaped by these ideological frames. A key difference between the frames of ARA and PI lies in how each group feels about being "colorblind."

WHAT'S WRONG WITH BEING COLORBLIND?

Before we look at the white antiracists' frames in depth, it may be useful to briefly discuss the topic of colorblindness and the powerful critique of it in much of the most recent scholarship on race in the United States. Liberals and conservatives alike hold up a colorblind ideal as the answer to racism, often using a popular line from Martin Luther King, Jr.'s, "I Have A Dream" speech to support their position. Yet King's words about judging people not by the color of their skin but by the content of their character are usually taken out of context to imply that King was against race-conscious policies and solutions for racism, when nothing could be further from the truth. In fact, King advocated race-based affirmative action based on the recognition of historical disadvantages faced by African Americans, stating that whites and blacks were not competing from the same starting line (Steinhorn and Diggs-Brown 2000). Today, colorblindness is seen as a way for the majority of white Americans to pretend like there is no more racism and to justify their lack of support for any further policy solutions for race-related problems. Being colorblind has been called an "evasive" position which ignores the color-stratified arrangements of American society. Such a position allows racism to survive and flourish—"central to the existence of racism is the politics of its denial"(Lubiano 1998, viii). Far from describing a utopia where racism would not exist, colorblindness could instead be a cover-up which allows racism to continue.

In her study of white women's racial ideologies, Ruth Frankenberg (1993) argued that colorblindness is the most common way whites deal with the issue of race today. She prefers to call it "color and power evasiveness," rather than colorblindness, because it is used to avoid confronting the existence of racial inequality and the power differentials inherent in such inequality. One of the hallmark phrases of those whites employing this discourse is "I don't care if he's black, brown, yellow, or green"—a "familiar cliché" which "camouflages socially significant differences of color in a welter of meaningless ones"(149). This "polite" language of race also masks ideas of white superiority. Those of her respondents who were "color and power evasive" prided themselves on not noticing color. Yet "the idea that noticing a person's color is not a good thing to do, even an offensive thing to do, suggests that 'color,' which here means nonwhiteness, is bad in and of itself"(145). When whites claim to not notice others' race, as in "I didn't even notice she was Black," there is an implicit ideology of white as the norm. Thus, whites' colorblind discourse places them in a privileged position where they are automatically at the top of a racial hierarchy, even as their language denies any existence of such a hierarchy. In order to become antiracist, whites must break with this dominant white colorblind discourse and employ a "race-cognizant" ideology. If they continue to be color and power evasive, this "short-circuits" antiracist action, keeping it at an introspective level (176). Frankenberg's study and others (see Feagin and Vera 1995) suggests that researchers should not expect to find *active* white antiracists using colorblind language. Surprisingly, in my research I did find colorblind discourse being used by some white antiracists, and this was directly related to organizational frames of racism, which I will outline in the following sections.

REFLEXIVE RACE COGNIZANCE

In concurrence with the previous literature, several of the white antiracist respondents interviewed for this project also rejected "colorblindness" as an ideology of antiracism. These respondents were all either PI members or nonorganizationally affiliated. Put most bluntly by David, a PI member: "If I claim colorblindness, I don't see how one can be antiracist. It's a contradiction." David and others spoke of colorblindness as incompatible with antiracism for a variety of reasons which can be divided into three main categories:

1. blindness to institutional racism;
2. blindness to others as people of color; and
3. blindness to self as white.

Although the respondents quoted in this section voiced their contempt for "colorblindness" as a solitary concept, it became clear from their testimony that what they were referring to was a multifaceted state of being which entailed blindness and "denial" of several issues.

Dimension One: Blindness to Institutional Racism

Racism is defined by Della Dora (1970) as "power plus privilege"—while privilege is something that occurs on an individual level, power is seen as something that operates on an institutional level. Under this conception, anyone can be prejudiced, but only those who hold the power (whites) can be racist, which discounts any notion of "black racism"(Feagin and Vera 1995). Several respondents agreed with this notion and did not see themselves as antiracist until they stopped being "blind" to institutional racism. Seeing racism as merely personal prejudice was looked upon by them as a naive, uninformed stance. Amy, an activist who once received death threats due to an antiracist action, made a distinction between becoming aware of racism as prejudice and being antiracist. Although her awareness was raised when she dated an African American boy in high school, she makes clear that she was not a true antiracist until much later.

> I thought I, in my head, had it all down—the whole, everybody's the same, we're all the same on the inside, you shouldn't be prejudiced against me if I'm not prejudiced against you, and blah, blah, whatever. That was the way I was thinking . . . I maintained that same viewpoint for quite a while . . . until I was a sophomore [in college] . . . I think it has to do with coming out, I think it has to do with taking women's studies . . . that was when I started being antiracist . . . when I started realizing, just when I started really understanding institutionalized racism, I think, is when I became antiracist. When I realized it wasn't a personal issue and it wasn't about you treat me the way I treat you and everybody's equal and blah, blah, blah, and we're all the same underneath. And I started realizing that being colorblind wasn't the way to go and stuff like that. Dropping the liberal ideology.

Here Amy noted that "dropping" colorblind discourse was in fact necessary in order for her to call herself an antiracist. For her, dropping colorblindness meant the shift from seeing racism as a "personal issue" to seeing it as an institutional issue. Elizabeth, who had also dated interracially as a teenager, referred to a similar personal transformation: "There was a time when I really subscribed to the belief that it would all be changed [laughs] if we all just joined hands. . . . And it's been recently . . . as I've grown up some I've realized that's not going to solve the whole thing . . . it's also structural." Here we see "colorblindness," in the form of seeing racism as a personal problem alone, being looked upon as silly and naive. Likewise, Kristin laughed at her early childhood awareness of racism; she thought she had solved the problem of the one black child in her class always being stared at when she saw a *3-2-1 Contact* episode in which it was pointed out that the only difference between her and this boy was the pigment in their skin. She laughed because she saw such colorblindness as overly idealistic from her newer race-cognizant perspective, or what she called her "political awakening." All three of these respondents bring out one dimension of "colorblindness"—the way in which whites tend to view the racial order as a whole, as an individual problem rather than a structural/institutional one. They did not see themselves as antiracist until they got rid of this "blind spot." Thus, one reason why respondents spoke of colorblindness as detrimental to antiracism is because it ignores the institutional nature of racism.

Dimension Two: Blindness to Others as People of Color

Pat Parker's poem "For the white person who wants to know how to be my friend" asks the reader to both forget and never forget that she is black, making the point that successful interracial intimacy should not be colorblind. Frankenberg (1993) argues that when whites "politely" pretend not to notice the race of someone different from themselves, it results in a feeling of superiority, as if one is overlooking a blemish or an imperfection. Several of my respondents also reflected negatively on whites' position of "not seeing" color. Rosalind, a member of PI, saw being colorblind as a way of ignoring racism as institutional power (Dimension One) but went on to talk about how that translated into ignoring the "color" of others:

> I think the colorblind thing is being used to pretend that people are not racist, and don't prejudge, and don't have power, and I think it's very insidious. [elsewhere:] And even if they did treat people the same, I think that when you look in terms of the institutions, that could be a very racist unfair thing to treat people the same. I think you have to treat people in terms of what they need and where they're coming from, that's more of a definition of fairness than treating people the same.

Referring to "treating people the same" as a part of colorblind ideology, which she went so far as to call racist, Rosalind reflected on the second dimension of colorblindness—not seeing people of color *as* people of color by recognizing the separate institutional realities that racism has created for them. Kendra, a PI member who has an African American husband, also distanced herself from a "colorblind" approach:

> I absolutely *do not* see myself as colorblind. I think that anyone who says they do is dishonest or confused. There's this t-shirt people wear and it says "love sees no color"—well, I think love *loves* all color. I think it's a very different thing. I think that "love sees no color" is denial, in this culture, in this racist culture.

Agreeing with Rosalind that "colorblindness" results in "denial" of racism, Kendra eloquently refers to two contrasting slogans that typify Frankenberg's two discourses—color and power evasive (love sees no color) versus race cognizant (love loves all color.) Her rejection of the colorblind stance is also based on the rationale that not seeing the "race" of others denies the existence of racism.

Pam, like her other PI colleagues, admitted she was not colorblind, mentioning that when she watches the news, she notices "color" when people of color are portrayed unfairly:

> I'm definitely not colorblind . . . you'd like to say you are, that it doesn't matter. But I think even in terms of a white antiracist, that's why—because now you have a better understanding of a different person's reality and where they're coming from and what they have to endure. So it's still there, but it matters for different reasons now.

Pam points out that as an antiracist she no longer notices "color" in a stereotypical manner (as a sign of inborn ability or lack thereof) but rather as a sign of what "they have to endure" (power differences.) In neither case would she categorize herself as color-blind, even though she recognizes the social desirability of doing so. Thus, in addition to representing ignorance of institutional racism, for these respondents colorblindness also meant denial of experiences of people of color in racist America.

Dimension Three: Blindness to Self as White

"Being white in this society almost by definition means rarely having to think about it"(Feagin and Vera 1995, 181). Feagin and Vera argue that this blindness allows whites to subscribe to the "sincere fiction" that there are no privileges or benefits that whites reap from the existence of white racism. Henry, a member of PI, explained how this white view of oneself in a way that does not acknowledge race can be problematic: "There's a great deal of denial and colorblindness that's in vogue, except I think it's being carefully done to shadow the reality of racism. . . . I mean, we define *what is* with our whiteness. And I think that needs to be addressed." Henry's focus on whites being definers of "what is" echoes Frankenberg's argument that the invisibility of whiteness gives it its power. In discussing this function of the "colorblind" view of self on the part of whites, PI member David stated,

> "I don't think of myself as white," that's what we get in the workshop all the time. Well, we try to say, and move people towards this: "That might be true, but others see you as that. And you can say whatever, but you need to know how you are being perceived. You also need to know that you represent a historical relationship. And until—not just until people know you, but until people see you doing some work and taking some risks and understanding some things, you're just going to be a representative of their experience with white folks.

Referring to PI Undoing Racism workshops, David's line of reasoning reflects DuBois's (1965) "double consciousness" idea—people of color have *had* to acknowledge the realities of both self and other in order to survive in racist America. Thus, as Henry put it, "Of course, it's been people of color that have had to know what it

means to be white even when we didn't." For whites, being blind
to whiteness means not being able to understand people of color's
perceptions of oneself, and that is seen by these respondents as a
stumbling block for the antiracist movement.

A sizable proportion of the sample unequivocally distanced
themselves from colorblindness and spoke of it as incompatible
with antiracism. They concluded this was so for three main reasons
or dimensions:

1. it avoids the existence of institutionalized racism;
2. it denies the meaning of "color" for people of color; and
3. it ignores "whiteness" as both the ability to be a "definer"
   and as a marker of historical and ongoing racism.

I call the discourse presented in this section *reflexive race cogni-*
zance because of dimensions two and three—"race" is seen as
something that is not just present for others who are racist, but is
inherent in the way the individual him- or herself views the self
and others. In the following section, I will present data which reveal some white antiracists who use colorblind language, though
not all three dimensions of colorblindness are used.

SELECTIVE RACE COGNIZANCE

Several scholars, and even the respondents quoted in the previous
section, have all claimed that "colorblindness" is incompatible
with aggressive white antiracism. Although Frankenberg does
identify some antiracists who mix race cognizance with color and
power-evasive language, she concludes that this is a crippling con-
coction that leaves people in a guilt-ridden mode without action.
The data presented here will pose a direct challenge to this assertion. Not only do the respondents quoted in this section use "colorblind" language at times, but those who tend to do so the most are
the members of the more action-oriented organization, ARA, and
have taken great risks to challenge racism in their communities.
Their reliance upon colorblind understandings at times has hardly
debilitated them or left them in an introspective state. Furthermore,
the colorblindness they use is not simultaneously blindness to all

three of the issues mentioned by the respondents in the previous section. They do not subscribe to institutional colorblindness (dimension one) but do sometimes use colorblindness to refer to themselves and others, perhaps distancing themselves from racism which has been framed as overt and "out there" by their group. Hence, I have categorized this usage of colorblindness as *selective race cognizance*, in contrast to the reflexive race cognizance used by PI members in the previous section.

When I asked Travis, an ARA member, to elaborate on his interracial relationship for which he claimed he was harassed (earlier in the interview), he responded in the following way:

> In terms of dating somebody of color, it really makes no difference if they're of color or not. I've dated people that are white, I date—it doesn't matter the color itself. . . . It's got nothin' to do with the pigment of your skin. . . . To me, there's racists in every nationality, every color, every religion, there's racists everywhere. . . . I've met hate-mongering people of every color and every nationality. It's the hatred itself that is the monster, the evil thing, right? . . . So there's hatred everywhere and there's good people everywhere. There's no thin line to say these people are and these people aren't—each person according to their merit alone.

Here Travis espoused the "love sees no color" colorblind view of others (dimension two), of which Kendra was so critical earlier. Then challenging the idea that only whites can be racist, Travis went on to say that hatred in any form could be considered racism, another "colorblind" position which respondents had claimed was denial of historical experiences of people of color. Examining this quote might lead one to assume that Travis, who discussed his colorblind views of others, must have also eschewed viewing himself as white or denied the institutional structures that benefit him. Yet elsewhere in the interview, he stated,

> The police would handle me different as they would somebody of color, the state would prosecute me different[ly] than they would somebody of color. I'm sure I get a little more leniency, because of the bigoted racist points of view of our police and the state, that I get a bit of lenience because I'm a white straight male.

Naming himself as a "white straight male," Travis switched to dimension one of the reflexive race-cognizant discourse when he pointed out the advantages he received from the government and its agencies because of its racist structure. Thus, even while Travis was "colorblind" on his view of others, he acknowledged the institutional realities of what his whiteness means in a racist system. Likewise, ARA member Jason articulated a colorblind view of himself and of others in the following quote:

> [on being white] It's that section on your driver's license that says skin color—that's about all it is to me. I'm not proud, I'm not not-proud, that's just the way I was born. When my page came up in the coloring book they whipped out the flesh [sic] colored crayon. And I'm not green, I'm not blue, I'm not any other color, I'm the color I was given. I look at everybody as human beings first, and that's really all that needs to be looked at.

Using what Frankenberg identifies as a common color and power evasive phrase, Jason referred to colors (blue, green) that are not part of our racial hierarchy, taking a colorblind view on his own whiteness (dimension three), as well as on the "color" of others (dimension two) in his last sentence. However, elsewhere in the interview, Jason was not "colorblind" on the institutional realities of whiteness and white privilege (dimension one):

> I know the shit that black people have to put up with, but I've never experienced it first hand. I've never been yanked out of a car by a cop because he suspects I'm in a gang or something like that. I've never been looked at twice by a group of people walking down the street. I've never been stereotyped on sight because of the way I look. . . . I haven't been put through 400 years of slavery and subjugation. I haven't been put through unlawful medical experiments that are still in fact going on.

While not using reflexive race-cognizant discourse, Jason did use Dimension One of it, by focusing on the institutional advantages that he receives from police, strangers, and the health care system, among other things. He and Travis both seemed to pride themselves on being colorblind as the right thing to do and posited racist institutions and their lack of colorblindness as the problem.

Perhaps the most powerful example of the complexity and multifaceted nature of colorblindness happened in the following exchange I had with Tim, an ARA member:

> I don't see myself as white, and I don't see other people as black, or Asian or whatever. I recognize the cultures, but as far as I'm concerned, we're all human . . . [me: I know you just told me that you don't see yourself as white, but what does it mean, do you think, generally speaking, to be white in this country?] It means that you have a better chance at a future, I guess. If you look at it in terms of the way it's been going in history, when you look in terms of race, white people quote founded this country and it's here for the white people or whatever, and they see themselves as better than other races, just cause of their skin or whatever. And, it just means you probably have a better chance than anyone else to go farther in your future . . . [me: mm-hm. Do you see yourself as part of that description that you just gave?] It's kinda hard not to, 'cause other than my social class, I am white. You can't change the color of your skin. You can change your consciousness of your skin color, but I'm still gonna have more of a chance, more—I can't think of the word right now—but I'm just gonna be able to do what I want more easily than if I was colored [sic], just based on that fact—which sucks, but, that's the way it is. And that's what we gotta break down and fight.

Here Tim captured powerfully the difference between being reflexive and selective about race by his hesitancy to use the pronoun "I" in certain statements. In his shift from first- to second-person pronouns, he started by professing a colorblind view of himself and others using the pronoun "I," but then shifted to using "you" and "they" when talking about historical and contemporary advantages for white people. When I did ask him to consider whether he included himself in that framework, he then oscillated between first and second person, pointing out that his "color" and how it is perceived is unalterable, but that he could at least change his own consciousness about it. Starting with a "colorblind" statement about himself and others, Tim revealed that he was not blind to institutional structures which benefited whites, even though it took probing for him to actually speak of himself as included in those benefits.

These data pose a direct challenge to the previous conceptions that white antiracists are uniformly noncolorblind. By breaking colorblindness into three different dimensions, we see that these individuals are not simply "not colorblind"—they both are and are not, depending on who's looking and how they are looking. The respondents in this section were not "colorblind" on dimension one, yet exhibited "colorblind" conceptions of race on dimensions two and/or three. Taking an "I'm OK, you're not OK" stance, they acknowledge the noncolorblind nature of our racist society yet see "colorblindness" as the preferred discourse for themselves. In recognizing racism on an institutional level but expressing "blindness" at the more local level of themselves and other people of color with whom they come into contact, these respondents exhibit a *micro* colorblindness but a *macro* awareness of racism (another way of defining *selective race cognizance.*)

This mix of "color and power evasive" discourse with "race cognizance" is something that Frankenberg (1993) found would forestall aggressive antiracist action, yet Travis, Jason, and Tim were hardly introspective or inactive. Travis lives in one city where neo-Nazis are quite territorial, and has found himself in both physical and verbal confrontations with racists, in successful struggles to keep the streets "hate free" and safe for people of all colors. Jason is one of the most active youth organizers for ARA in his city, coordinating the electronic (E-mail and Internet) media of the group as well as participating regularly in Copwatch street monitoring. Tim was one of the leaders of the outspoken opposition to white supremacist-led "White Power Hour" TV show on his local cable access station. He narrowly escaped arrest when he and some others staged a protest outside the apartment of the show's host. He credits the actions of himself and his ARA colleagues with raising awareness about the presence of racist hate and violence in his community. These activists' partially colorblind, or selectively race-cognizant, views have hardly kept them at an inactive pace.

Because Frankenberg's race relations based theory did not take into account the possibility of the frames of different social movement organizations influencing the outcomes, she was not able to predict such an antiracist use of colorblindness. As table 3.1 illustrates, while there can be a racist use of colorblindness (bottom left cell) as Frankenberg and Carr (1997) argue, there can also be an antiracist use of colorblindness, which is *selective* race cognizance (top left cell) as presented in this section. This acknowledges racism as an institutional problem that needs to be addressed, yet

Table 3.1   Uses of "Colorblind" Discourse

		Colorblind	
		Yes	No
Antiracist	Yes	Selective race cognizance (ARA)	Reflexive race cognizance (PI)
	No	Color and power evasive/ "nonracist"	Overt racist/white supremacist

not as a problem of oneself or the way oneself sees others. This is compatible with the framing of ARA. In contrast, reflexive race cognizance (top right cell) is an antiracist rejection of colorblindness along all three of its dimensions. The bottom right cell is a reminder that colorblindness can also be rejected in a racist way (i.e., "I see 'color' differences and they should be used as a basis for discrimination"), which would be an overt form of racism. Neither of the bottom two (non-antiracist) cells represent language used by the respondents in this book.

FRAMING AND ORGANIZATIONAL STRATEGY
Framing Colorblindness

Organizational culture and the organizations' framing of what an antiracism movement should be clearly affects the extent to which they engage with "colorblind" discourse. Those who spoke predominantly in a "reflexive race-cognizant" manner (explicitly opposed to "colorblindness") were either nonorganizationally affiliated antiracists or members of PI. When they were not members of organizations (i.e., Amy) they seemed to obtain their cognitive ideologies about race through academic writing, and as we have seen, the scholarly writings concur with Frankenberg's race-cognizant position. For PI members, it is an outcome of their organizational framing that they are thoughtfully reflective about their own positions of whiteness and their role in racism. The Undoing Racism workshops—of which all the respondents here had attended at least one (and usually more than one)—are explicit in putting forth that all whites are racist by definition, and that colorblindness is a form of denial and escapism from the reality of racism. PI's master frame of the problem of racism is one that posits whites, and the institutional power that they hold, as the antagonists. PI also focuses its workshops towards people who are already working at progressive social change (e.g, educators in poor communities, peace activists, social service agencies and churches), since their project is the Undoing of Racism in these more subtle areas, rather than targeting overt hate groups like the KKK. As such, PI's diagnostic frame of the problem is "we are the problem"—accepting this during the workshop is often an emotionally trying time for many whites. This framing makes it virtually impossible for them to take the "I'm OK, you're not OK" stance (one form of colorblindness) taken by members of other antiracist organizations. Even the very structure of the organization, with its separate group for whites (European Dissent), creates an atmosphere where "color" simply cannot be ignored. Thus, it is clear that when one's organization frames racism as a problem of subtle inequities in which all whites play a role, and separates members accordingly, reflexive race cognizance, or absence of all colorblindness, is likely to result.

Alternatively, other white antiracists take a selectively race-cognizant position. They recognize the institutional structure of racism and the historical and contemporary advantage that has been given to whites, but fail to reflect on themselves as whites and others as people of color in any meaningful way when considering them as individuals. They pride themselves on being colorblind but recognize that others—hateful people and institutions—are not. Further, their master frame posits that these noncolorblind, discriminatory others *are* the antagonist. They do not see themselves as also the antagonists, as PI members would. Organizational affiliation is again relevant here since all the respondents here who fit into this category were members of ARA. This organization's educational publications and its actions themselves point toward *overt* racists as the antagonists. Most of their writings and actions focus on white power groups as the antagonists, such as the culprits of the black church bombings and the Oklahoma City bombings.

A poignant pictorial illustration of ARA's diagnostic framing of the racism problem is on the back cover of the January 1998 issue of *ARA News*. There is a hooded Klansman with several kids scowling up at him, and the caption reads, "Ew, gross! Let's call ARA!"

Clearly, overt racists like KKK members are the antagonist, and ARA is the protagonist. Although the assailants ("bad guys") here and in all cases mentioned in *ARA News* are identified as white people (ARA does *not* participate in the "black racism" idea,) nowhere is it asserted that only whites can be racist, or that whites as an entire group are the problem. ARA's mission statement says it rejects hate in any form (including sexism, homophobia, anti-Semitism, etc.), and as Travis noted, "hatemongers" come in every "color." ARA is not structurally separated by race, as is PI. All ARA members meet together, regardless of race (although people of color in the group are a small minority.) Tasks and goals are not identified in any racially specific way, as with PI where white members are told they have work to do which is quite different from that which people of color should do. Thus, a frame which shows "blindness" towards its members' race even as it recognizes the color of antagonists, coupled with the framing of blatant acts of hostility as the main targets of antiracist activism, creates an atmosphere in which Selective Race Cognizance (a form of color-blindness) is fostered. In this atmosphere, this specific kind of colorblindness is not incompatible with the tasks and goals at hand (fighting overt racist practices) and it is not at all debilitating to action.

The target audience is relevant here as well. Since PI frames leftist organizers and nonprofit agencies as its target audience, it has less of a hurdle to overcome than ARA whose focus is often toward a younger, more mainstream crowd. Because colorblindness is the dominant white discourse on race, a group that incorporates (selectively) this way of thinking in its materials has a better hope of reaching a larger more mainstream audience, as ARA does, by speaking its language.

Strategizing Colorblindness

This raises the question of colorblindness being used as a strategy. It should be clear that colorblindness is not simply something one is or is not (as in a noun) but rather can be conceptualized as an adjective to describe certain ways of thinking and discussing ideologies about race. The categories are not static, but shifting at

times, and situational. Thus, one person could be located in different cells of this table at different times, even as an ARA or PI member. For instance, Pam, a PI member, characterized herself as
"definitely not colorblind," but she did engage with using colorblindness in the following quote:

> If this were a perfect world, you could reach utopia where color didn't
> matter in jobs or whatever, but history is there . . . you have to respect
> the history that came before, and understand it. . . . I think for some-
> body who is colorblind in the negative sense of the word, I want to
> work from the negative colorblind to the positive colorblind. . . . There
> should be a shift in the definition.

For Pam, using colorblindness in a "positive" way meant that she
would "appreciate who you are . . . regardless of color." When she
talked about appreciating people, she was referring to different
histories of power and culture, yet using colorblindness to say she
would regard those distinct histories in an equal way for all. Pam
was incorporating the dominant language of colorblindness as an
ideal point into her own reflexive race-cognizant philosophy. She
wanted a "shift in the definition" that would be antiracist yet still
use popular colorblind language—a "positive colorblind."
    ARA member Mac also wanted to work with the dominant col-
orblind discourse yet still impart an antiracist message to a potential ARA member. The night I was "tabling" (passing out ARA
literature, soliciting with a sign-up sheet) with Mac, a curious
white boy approached the table tentatively, asking Mac if ARA
also focused on "black racism." Expecting Mac to rattle off the
sociological definition of "power + prejudice = racism" and explain how only white people can be racist, I was surprised at what
happened instead. Mac assured the boy that ARA was against hate
in *any* form. Mac picked up a copy of *ARA News*, showing him
a quote from Muhammad Ali, who stated that he regretted any
antiwhite feelings he had as an early Black Muslim. Yet Mac then
turned the pages of the newsletter to reveal a preponderance of
newspaper clippings collected that month on racist violence, all of
it white-on-black. He mentioned that while ARA condemns hate
in any form, they have noticed no black group that even approaches the equivalent of the KKK and other white groups with

genocidal missions. This boy, who was not going to sign up on the mailing list before this exchange, then signed his name and picked up some information. Mac told me it was crucial that ARA not appear "hypocritical" in claiming that one group can be racist and another cannot, because they want to get people's "foot in the door" so to speak ("hey, come join this fun organization!"), to then hear their larger message. Mac said that many of these kids are just as likely to go to a neo-Nazi group instead if their initial message sounds more consistent. This is why he feels it imperative that ARA not take an aggressively race-cognizant stance up front, but rather send the message more subtly in presenting the evidence of a white racist society through their publications, and allow them to draw their own conclusions.

Both Pam and Mac, regardless of organizational affiliation, referred to colorblindness as a strategy, a way of "shifting definitions" so that the "message" of antiracism could be better understood on a larger scale. It was a part of their movement-building ideology. The point here is that organizational frames are not proscriptive—ARA members do not always adhere to colorblindness, and PI members do not always avoid it. Colorblindness can sometimes be used as a tool to engage with the larger white culture which obviously adheres to this way of thinking about race and race relations.

IMPLICATIONS OF THE EXISTENCE OF
MULTIPLE ANTIRACISMS

One of the more popular frameworks for types of white thinking about race has been that of Ruth Frankenberg, yet here I have challenged her assertion that colorblindness is incompatible with white antiracist action, since my data show otherwise. Organizations that frame overt acts of racism as their main focus of activism and thus do not see themselves, as whites, as antagonists often use selective race cognizance. Under this way of thinking about race, one can use color and power evasive (colorblind) discourse about oneself and others, yet still be cognizant and vigilant about institutionalized racism in day to day life. Because Frankenberg only included a few antiracist whites in her sample, and did not investigate any organizational memberships in detail, it is understandable that she did not find such variation.

What does this mean for building a successful white antiracist movement? As Blauner (1995) has argued, the "white radical" language of race, or what I have labeled as reflexive race cognizance typical of PI members, can be seen as detrimental to antiracist coalition building. Positing whites as the antagonists because they are white, as reflexive race cognizance does, often alienates the majority of whites who believe racism is a personal character flaw rather than something all whites inherited by virtue of the history of our culture. If white antiracists desire large scale cultural change, Blauner recommends they change their language so they can speak to the dominant culture more effectively, without putting them on the defensive. While I think Blauner goes too far by accusing white radicals of being the PC police (excessively monitoring "politically correct" terminology) and by suggesting we abandon the concept of racism altogether, he makes the important point that multiple white antiracist discourses need to develop in order to take into account that the majority of whites still think in colorblind ways about race. Those who use selective race cognizance do this by relying on certain colorblind concepts that are popular with the dominant culture (i.e., Jason: "I look at everybody as human beings first, and that's really all that needs to be looked at") while still bringing racism to the forefront as an institutionalized social problem. The practice of selective race cognizance as described in this study presents a more antiracist alternative for behavior than abandoning the concept of racism altogether, which is the only tangible suggestion in Blauner's essay.

Even members of PI, a more reflexively race cognizant organization, acknowledge the need to develop a more accessible way of thinking about antiracism. For example, Rosalind remarked: "I don't even use the word racist unless I'm talking to somebody who's been through the training because I know that their definition will be so far from mine, that I'd have to do a whole training [for them] to get the definition." Mike, another PI member, also reflected on the discrepancy between the reflexive race cognizant view that his organization espouses and that of other white people:

One of the things that we've worked real hard on is to try to create a language to discuss antiracist ideas with other white people. And we're finding that it's something that just has been done so infrequently, that it's really challenging. It's a very big struggle to talk about being antiracist with other white people.

Since antiracism for Mike as a PI member inherently means a reflexively race cognizant ideology, he described it as "really challenging" to impart that knowledge to other white people who are undoubtedly operating from some variant of a colorblind framework. Thus, the existence of multiple white antiracisms, on the one hand, clearly opens up the possibility for incorporating more and more whites into the movement, just by having different ways to talk to other whites.

On the other hand, however, there is the concern that white antiracists who are not constantly reflective about their own involvement in racist structures will inadvertently perpetuate racism even as they participate in antiracist work. One black antiracist, who resides in the same city where a large chapter of ARA is active, was adamant on this point:

> Oftentimes in spaces that were supposed to be positive antiracist spaces, I have had a hard time differentiating between the racist and antiracist. I look for that self-analysis. What needs to be examined is white culture. That is what needs to be examined. You wouldn't have this racism, the racism is a result of white culture. So until that is examined and dismantled which they have a very difficult time doing. For the most part if you ask a white person what does it mean to be white they will tell you everything that it isn't. They will not tell you what it is. Until they do that we have no hope. They can't even admit most of the time that they are privileged. So until the majority is willing to admit their privileges and then examine those and give up a little control then there is no hope for racism.

Since selective race cognizance (typical of ARA) involves blindness to oneself as white, it could be that even as ARA increases its membership and fights neo-Nazi and police brutality, its members still perpetuate racism by this lack of "self-analysis" described above. How organizations frame the issue of racism is not simply a matter of semantics. As we will see in the subsequent chapters on white antiracist actions, the reflexive race cognizance typical of PI members results in more contemplation of the effects of their actions.

There are several different concepts and standards by which PI members in particular evaluate their work, which often distinguishes them from other white antiracists. The question then essentially becomes whether the higher numbers of people that selective engagement with colorblindness brings is more important than the overall effectiveness that reflective race cognizance brings. A review of the data on white antiracist activities in the following chapters will bring us closer to answering this question.

WHAT SHOULD I SAY?—
INDIVIDUAL ANTIRACIST STRATEGIES

At some level, you recognize the white bonding and either you avoid it or you call it. . . . In some way as a white person I always have the privilege of not doing this work. . . . Even though it ultimately is not [an option for me] but I have to acknowledge that I can avoid it if I want. . . . Sometimes [my response is] getting angry, sometimes it's just making my statement, sometimes it's trying to get someone to talk and talk about where they are and really listen. . . . Some of that work takes a long period of time, and often in an instant all you can do is say something with the hopes that they're going to at least around you not do it again but also think about what they're saying. . . . I think the other thing to do is after something happens [is to ask yourself] what response did you make and how satisfied were you with the result of that response?

Here Paul touched upon the many issues and strategies white antiracists consider when deciding "what can I do?" His statement reiterates the core theme of this book that there are many different ways to proceed in the work, and that his whiteness indeed plays a role in those options. Because these options are so numerous, I have devoted two chapters to explore the range of white antiracist actions. Drawing upon Carmichael and Hamilton (1967), Feagin and Feagin (1996) explain that racism occurs on two main levels—individual and institutional. For the purposes of this study, I have followed this individual/institutional distinction by choosing to deal with individual or microlevel antiracism in this chapter, and with institutional or macrolevel antiracism in a subsequent chapter. This division for matters of convenience is in no way meant to obscure the interrelated nature of these two "levels" of racism. Philomena Essed (1991) who advocates the more holistic notion of "everyday racism" notes that this individual/institutional dichotomy "places the individual outside the institutional," (36) as if individuals did not create and maintain institutions. Thus, "the term individual racism is a contradiction in itself because racism is by definition the expression or activation of group power" (37). So when white antiracists encounter other whites practicing racism in everyday interactions, they are not merely facing differences in personal opinion, but are actually dealing with differences in how they, as individuals, activate systemic power and privilege. The accounts provided here are no exception to this rule.

Although there is no social science research exploring the methods whites use to confront everyday racism, there are two studies which examine how blacks confront such incidents. First, the work of Feagin (1991) on middle-class African Americans shows that they deal with discrimination from whites in a number of different ways—withdrawal/exit, resigned acceptance, verbal response, and physical counterattack. Although a verbal response was the most common, the decision not to confront and simply walk away from the situation was also common, due to concerns about playing into white stereotypes of the "oversensitive" black person. To avoid the stigma of this stereotype, blacks often used their "second eye"—an extra evaluation of a situation to make certain someone's intentions were racially motivated before they act. Similarly, Essed's (1991) research on black women's experiences with discrimination notes that one's choice of retaliation strategy varies depending on the situation, especially what the counterreaction of the whites will be. The worry that whites will counteract with the charge of "oversensitivity" is not unfounded. Many of the women of color in this study were accused of "exaggerating," of "jumping to conclusions," or even of being racist themselves when they chose to challenge everyday racism (274). So the "second eye" becomes yet another burden for people of color in a white dominated society—they must take extra time to second-guess themselves for fear of further white retaliation.

Since whites are in a very different position, however, it is not likely that their actions will be identical. Because whites are not the targets of the racism that they are challenging as antiracists, the opportunities for action available to them are quite different. Although they also can directly challenge a discriminatory act against a person of color that they witness, they additionally can be present when whites commit racist speech and actions they would do in the company of other whites only[1]—an arena to which people of color do not have access. However, they are less likely to face the accusations of bias and oversensitivity that people of color face when pointing out racism to other whites. Whites may also be less likely to retaliate by calling a white person who confronts them "racist" because they are addressing a member of their own race. Does this mean that the white antiracist's task is much easier, and that she or he can proceed no holds barred, with little strategy to speak of? Unfortunately, the answer is a bit more complex. White antiracist actions at the individual level range along a continuum of strategies, and these whites often give careful thought to which strategy they will use in any given instance. As we shall see, these strategies range from immediate vocal opposition to saying nothing at all. Further, being white and cognizant of their privileges, some of these antiracists called into question their use of extreme strategies—either extreme directness or extreme complacency—as forms of racism themselves, and described ways to keep this in check.

INTERRUPTING RACISM

When I asked the respondents what actions they did that they would identify as antiracist, a common response was that they made problematic the everyday racist comments of other whites. They all had their own names for this action; Pierce called it having "political discussions," Elizabeth called it "preaching to other white people," and Susan called it "interrupting" the normal flow of white business-as-usual to challenge or confront white conversational racism. Although respondents' terminology varied, for the purposes of this analysis I have categorized these actions at the individual level as confrontations or challenges. Confrontations refer to instances when, within the time and space of an incident, an antiracist brings to a white person's attention the racist impact of their speech and/or action. Challenges are more subtle ways of making one's opposition known, usually by countering with some positive statement about people of color or policies which benefit them. ARA member Holly gave one example of a confrontation:

> When people are being really bigoted, I usually say something, even on a streetcar; that's happened a couple of times. [me: really?] These two women were talking. This woman was *horrible,* she was just talking to her friend like about how the whole neighborhood was changing and all these Chinese people, and it doesn't feel like Canada anymore and stuff. And then she just started talking about welfare bums or something. I just started giving her shit, and I just thought, it was embarrassing her a lot, and using swear words and things like that, it was really good! They get so discombobulated. And she's like, "how dare you talk to me like that?" And I was like: "Well, how dare you go and spew this on the streetcar—this is public space! Go ahead, say that in your own house, I don't care what you think. But, you're making all these people uncomfortable, including me!"

Doing what Susan called "interrupting," Holly surprised another white person who felt free to carry on a racist conversation around her by expressing disagreement. This confrontation was quite direct and vocal, done in a public way, and directed at a stranger.

Kristin had a chance to confront the racist comments of a family friend, so her approach was a bit more diplomatic. This German friend owned a restaurant which participated in a program to hire rehabilitated juvenile offenders, and she just happened to place all of the predominantly black people from that program in the lowest paying dishwasher positions. Kristin described her friend's response when she was asked about this racist practice:

> "Well, they're all too lazy, and so we can't afford to have them out front because they'll mess up, because they'll just stand back and they won't even serve people properly and that kind of thing." And so I asked, "Well, what do you mean they're all too lazy?" And she said, "Well, you know, black people are lazy!" You know, nudging me and being like, "Come on, Kristin, you know that, don't you, you must know that?" [And, I said:] "[her name], you're making a huge generalization

by saying that. What if I said, all Germans are fascist Nazis, do you think that would be a fair statement?" And so of course she immediately felt kind of stupid [laughs] because I wasn't saying, "Oh, yeah, of course, all black people are lazy." [Instead] I was like [actually] thinking! But, so that would be my example. She really didn't have a lot to say about it; I think she very quickly found something really important to do and had to leave [laughs].

This account further illustrates how whites expect other whites to go along with racist ideology, even physically nudging those who would be apathetic or indifferent into complying. One of the types of white antiracist action is indeed to challenge this dominant white mode of interaction. This "interruption" is quite similar to Garfinkel's breaching experiments (Heritage 1984) in which the everyday, taken-for-granted pattern of "hi, how are you" interactions is interrupted, throwing the participants off guard. Kristin's confrontation directly followed the remark, and disrupted the pattern of agreement that seemed to be expected of her.

Interrupting, or breaching, conversational racism can take different forms. Lisa, PI member, described how she challenged the racist comment of a ninety-nine-year-old woman in her church:

The church where I had started attending here is integrated and so I went in with a lot of basic assumptions like, wow, I mean, that's rare, in and of itself [laughs] in a city. And I had been church shopping for six months and totally restless. I had been going a few weeks or whatever, an older lady who just turned a hundred last month—which clues you into like what school of thought she's coming from—but I sat beside her the one Sunday. Right before the pastor got up, she leans over to me, and she's like, "Oh, honey, we're so glad you're coming to this church," she was like, "It's really dying, it's on its last legs and you know, you can help save the church," she's like, "The blacks are takin' over!" and said it loud enough that the mother with her two kids behind me [could hear] and it just floored me! I just didn't expect it at all, she's the nicest lady, blah, blah blah. She said this, and boom, the pastor was up at the podium and I'm like feeling like I'm gonna get up and move, but at the same time, understanding that this woman at the time was 99 years old and—whatever, all that stuff. And so, little incidences like that that happen a lot that people just assume, whatever. But, after the service, then, I did talk to her and I was just like, "One of the reasons I really love this church is because, you know, all the diversity and

culture" and blah, blah, blah, and she just looked at me with her mouth
open and didn't [laughs] really say a whole lot.

Like Kristin, Lisa was approached as if, since she was white, she
would be in sympathetic understanding of a racist ideology. Although she was not immediately able to confront the comment, she
made sure to challenge the sentiment that racial diversity was a
bad thing later on in her conversation with the old woman.

These three anecdotes also bring out the diversity of range of
responses to individual racism. In Holly's case, a rather vocal dissi-
dence, including profanity, was expressed. These were people she
did not know and would probably not see again. In Kristin's case,
with a friend of the family, she chose to draw on "overlapping
approximations" to solicit understanding of racism by using an
analogy to the woman's German ancestry and stereotypes that
could be made about her. In both of those two situations, the confrontation occurred directly when the comments were being made.
Lisa, taking the age of the woman who had made the racist comment into account, made it clear in a positive and even cheerful
way that she embraced the diversity that the woman so arduously
condemned. Challenging, rather than confronting, the woman was
something that happened in a delayed fashion because the start of
the church service made it so she was unable to do it directly.
These accounts make the point that there are many different ways
to interrupt or breach conversational racism, whether direct or delayed, confrontation or challenge. The chosen strategy often depends upon evaluation of the situation—specifically considering,
how close is this person to the antiracist and what potential is there
for change.

STRATEGIC CONFRONTATION—CHOOSING BATTLES

Several respondents described this strategic evaluation process for
how to confront individual acts of racism. Mac, ARA member and
organizer, described the range of actions he chooses for dealing
with conversational racism, including not interrupting it at all:

> I'm a real practical person and I don't try to convince anyone beyond
> the amount I think I can. . . . I am more skilled as a revolutionary now

than I was when I believed that every time somebody said "nigger" I had to throw a fit. I don't have to do anything, except whatever is the most effective right then to get them closer to fixing it. So, if shutting your mouth and walking out is the smartest thing—well, actually, if any other choice will create more harm than good—then your responsibility as a revolutionary is to shut your mouth, smile, act like you didn't hear it, and move on, because we have to win. We can't be just making stands in the abstract and being unpopular. We have to get people's ideas to change, and ranting sometimes pushes them the other way. . . . How I react to it is essentially whatever is my perception of what's most effective at the time. It could vary from picking up a lead bar and striking the perpetrator [laughs] to smiling, laughing at a racist joke, turning around, going outside and puking where no one can see me. It varies.

Mac made it clear that his evaluation process includes assessing the situation and deciding which response would be the most effective in terms of getting someone's ideas to change. Because "ranting sometimes pushes them the other way," he sometimes opts for little or no confrontation, but does not rule out more aggressive confrontation when it would be effective.

Nancy spoke of a similar evolution in her thinking about how aggressively she needed to confront instances of conversational racism. She said, "When you're new at it . . . you're always running around judging people and intervening in ways that are embarrassing and hurtful." But now, like Mac, she is more strategic, and she gave an example from her recent past to illustrate how that plays out in a specific situation:

I think that we have to evaluate and choose our battles. First of all, they don't need to be battles. I used to think I needed to say [in pompous tone:], "You're being a racist! blah, blah, blah," instead of saying, "Could you come here for a second? Do you realize that there are ten people"—because this just happened to me the other day—"that there are ten people in this line, five African American and five white, they all handed you a credit card, you handed the credit cards back to the white people and you put the black people's credit cards down on the counter? Do you know you did that? Do you know how it looks, how it feels to me?" You know, and try to save the person's dignity, and doing it, hope they behave differently. As opposed to before [I might have said:], "I'm so fucking sick of standing here watching you slam black people's cards down!" And three of the black people were in such

denial that they didn't even notice it! And now I've embarrassed everybody! . . . I never learned anything with a speeding bus bearing down
on me, and if my goal is really to change something, I could do it in a
kinder way. I sound like George Bush! [said disgustedly] A kinder gen-
tler way [laughs]. . . . [But] who am I to punish someone else when I
know that I'm walking around with unconscious racism too? And why
can't I give them an example of being able to say to me, "Thank you, I
never thought of it that way." Because that's what I want to learn to do
when people confront me about my mistakes, is say, "Thank you, your
criticism is a gift, and I accept the gift," where before I always had to
defend myself.

Like Mac, Nancy considers the end goal of antiracist action, which
is to "really change something," and tries to keep that goal in mind
when considering how she responds to an event. Also, part of her
strategy involves putting herself in the shoes of the white person
she is confronting, and considering which approach would be most
influential to her. Here she chose a calm confrontation which she
delayed until most of the other people in the setting were out of
earshot.

PI member Lisa shared Nancy's conviction that a knee-jerk reaction is not always the most effective:

For me, now, it's all about being strategic about what I say and how I
respond. Because I know that most of the times it would be with a
white person that I had an ongoing relationship with, and if they say
something that I'm uncomfortable with, it might not be the right setting
to respond now. But I know that down the road, there's gonna be an
opportunity for me. And it'll let me formulate a more effective response
if I don't necessarily just [snaps] react on the spot. So I'm much more
strategic.

Calling it strategic, Lisa shared Mac's concern for taking the setting
into account and formulating the most fitting response given that
information. Another PI member, Rosalind, stated that she too may
forgo reacting to a racist comment right away, in hopes of establishing a more lasting connection with that person that she feels
might be more influential:

I'm thinking about one of my conversations with [name] who used to
be my boss at the counseling center. She went through the [PI Undoing

Racism] training and hated it, never got over it, got angrier and angrier about it. What I do with most people who are coming from a very racist place—and maybe this is the therapist in me—but I just listen. And if I see a little place where I can question or put in a little bit of new information, introduce a new angle, then I'll try to inject it, but I'm not at all aggressive in trying to change somebody's mind. . . . I haven't had any success with that. . . . I want people to let me in on their world, and I'm afraid that if I attack their world too quickly or too strongly, that that'll be the end of any real communication.

Rosalind's concern about getting through to other whites means that sometimes the best action is no action at all. Her initial response was a fairly neutral one. Yet instead of reacting to her own behavior by saying, "I wish I would have said something," she saw what might have been interpreted as inaction as part of a larger, more long-term action plan.

Another factor that could have contributed to Rosalind's strategy for this particular situation is that the person in question was her boss. Power relations among whites, especially in the workplace, can affect the extent to which an individual white person can make change in a conversation. As Joel put it, "My boss sits there and gripes and bitches about affirmative action because it holds up her hands to hire and fire and stuff like that. But what can I do except to say, 'I think it's a good thing.' [laughs] She don't give a rat's ass what I think!" In saying affirmative action is "a good thing," Joel did directly challenge his boss, by countering her negative with a positive, but he was rather dissatisfied by its limited effectiveness, given the power differential between them.

The striking thing about white antiracists' accounts of situations in which they did not say much of anything when a racist comment was being made is that they do not tend to express regret over whatever they did not say. Rather, they see it as part of an overall strategy in their lives to "choose the battles" where they realistically think they could be most influential. Take the example of PI member Pam, a school teacher who said nothing when an overtly racist comment was made by a coworker:

A bunch of us from school went up to a bar, and we don't like this person anyway, but that's beside the point. We're sitting there, and [I'm sitting with] someone I work with [who] is biracial, I think obviously so—very light, but nonetheless it's obvious, and it's not like it was the first time she—this other person—ever met him. I mean, he works practically next door to them. And she said that one of the children on the playground came up to her and said that this little boy's mama does drugs. And she said [to the child], "Oh, you shouldn't talk like that." But to us, she's saying, "Well, of course she does, and you know what? She likes to sleep with black men!" [pause] And my friend and I just looked at each other and we didn't know what to say. And he just got up and left. And here we were, first-year teachers, we were never in this school before—I think it's been like two months that we'd been in that school. What were we gonna say? Were we gonna drive that wedge right then and there? Do you let it go? You can't excuse it, and every time I look at her, I see that.

Pam made clear her disapproval of the racist comment in her conversation with me, her biracial friend made clear his disapproval by leaving, and it is not clear whether Pam then did the same. But clearly she implicated her work situation as the reason she did not confront the remark orally. What is notable about Pam's situation is that some of her most effective antiracist actions have been done at her school, including creating institutional change by creating a multicultural arts program. (See chapter 5 for more on institutional antiracism.) Had she jeopardized her work situation during the bar incident, she might never have been able to have such an antiracist influence at her job. So as in Rosalind's case, Pam's inaction in this particular incident can be seen as a strategy—a part of a more long-term plan of antiracist action.

While white antiracists sometimes choose to confront or challenge racist speech and/or actions directly, others (described in this section) talk about delayed strategies that involve either taking the person to the side in private or waiting until a more opportune time. Although Nancy's account referred to someone she did not know (a cashier), most of the activists who mentioned strategizing were thinking of people with whom they had ongoing relationships. In these cases, particularly those that were work-related, the respondents tried to visualize themselves making changes over the long term rather than aggressively confronting the person right away. This picture of the strategizing antiracist activist certainly stands in stark contrast to the stereotype of the "PC (politically correct) police"—always waiting to jump on any transgression at

Table 4.1 Continuum of Individual Antiracist Strategies

Type 1 Holly	Type 2 Kristin, Kendra Nancy		Type 3 Joel Lisa		Type 4 Pam, Rosalind, Henry
Direct	Direct	Delayed	Direct	Delayed	Delayed
Angry confrontation	Calm confrontation using reasoning against racial bias; teacher role		Challenge using positive statements about people of color or antiracist policies		In favor of later, more influential action

every turn. The ideal of the activist who is never silent in the face of injustice was seldom present in their conceptualizations of antiracist action. Yet it is important to note that even when respondents did not confront or challenge a perpetrator immediately, they were far from ignoring or excusing the behavior. They did the best they could to plant seeds that would get people thinking, or took steps to position themselves so that they would be more effective at a later date. These strategies can be envisioned along the continuum depicted in table 4.1.

While these strategies have overall effectiveness as the primary concern, and one's relationship to the perpetrator was an important factor in determining overall effectiveness, these decisions do not occur in a vacuum where the race of those involved is neutral. Taking into consideration their own whiteness was an important part of developing their action strategies, as we will see in the following section.

PRIVILEGED RESISTANCE

When white antiracists express their concerns about being strategic in confronting everyday racism, they often locate those concerns within their specific context of being white. Kendra, for example, talked about being strategic in deciding what people could "hear," and how being socialized into white culture often affects whether we take the time to make that assessment:

> How direct I am with people about racism, it's something [where] I have to sense what they can hear, and I really try to, but I always will

try to say something that they *can hear*. What I *don't* think is helpful is—I think it's a luxury for white people, white antiracist activists—and I've gotten caught in this, I've seen others get caught in this—it's a luxury for us to get angry and indignant, and cuss somebody out for saying stupid things. And I think we have to speak out and take a stand, but I think that when we do that, I think we sometimes step over into being arrogant ourselves, and we are careless about the way we do it. I think that we have to really determine whether or not somebody can hear, what they can hear, and say something that they *hear*, if we wanna make a difference.

Speaking of strategic assessment as a particular challenge for whites, Kendra pointed out that whites have the luxury of being able to be more vocally confrontational about racism with fewer personal repercussions than people of color would expect to face for the same actions. I call this *privileged resistance*. Several other respondents made this privileged position with respect to actions very clear. Lori, for example, remarked that "if a person of color expresses an antiracist opinion, they're just being overly sensitive," yet, as a white person with privilege, people would "listen to me more" because she is a member of the dominant group. Amy, along with Kristin and Olivia (of ARA), also pointed out that whites could take more risks at marches and demonstrations and be less likely to get arrested.

It is widely acknowledged among antiracists that whites are taken more seriously when talking about racism than are people of color, just as feminists know that men are taken much more seriously than are women when they are talking about sexism. Yet there is not much in the academic literature about this matter. Peggy McIntosh (1998) has been cited widely for her piece on white privilege, and her itemized list of privileges she enjoys because she is white includes: "If I declare there is a racial issue at hand, or there isn't a racial issue at hand, my race will lend me more credibility for either position than a person of color will have" (98). Yet there has been no systematic analysis of how one's race affects one's credibility and effectiveness when challenging racism. *Privileged resistance* thus refers to the greater range of strategies white antiracists can use because of white privilege. They are less likely to be seen as "angry blacks" with "chips on their shoulders." By naming this *privileged resistance*, I am giving voice to something which many anti-oppression activists have known for quite some time, but which has not been adequately dealt with in social science literature.

This privileged position is not without its pitfalls, however, and Kendra's earlier quote attests to this. Because people of color have often had to suffer grave consequences for speaking out against racism, they tend to be more strategic about "choosing their battles" (Feagin 1991; Feagin and Sikes 1994), whereas whites, if paying too little attention to being strategic, could lose their overall effectiveness. Thus, Kendra said that, when possible, she takes her cue from people of color on how to respond. She chose the following anecdote from her life to illustrate this point:

> One night I was sitting at the dinner table with my [black] husband and my [white] stepmother and my little daughter, and we needed some napkins. And my little brother was in the other room and I said, "[Name], will you grab me a napkin?" Then [he] came into the room with a roll of paper towels. And my mother says, "[Name], there's napkins in there, come on, let's eat like the white folks." [pause] And [laughs] [my husband] and I are looking at her, you know? And she's like, "Oh, I'm so sorry, I'm so sorry," and she said, " Oh, I spent too many years hanging around your father." So she was blaming it on him and [laughs] I said, "Well, that wasn't him, that was *you, you* said that!" [laughs] . . . This friend of mine I was telling her, and she said, "Well, did you just get up and walk out?" And I said, "No." I said, "if [my husband] had wanted to get up and walk out, we would've." But I didn't throw a temper tantrum at her. I did make sure that she knew what she'd said, and she did know what she'd said. But I think to have acted out and thrown a temper tantrum and gotten up and walked out, I don't think it would have changed her. I think that having her realize that she had just hurt someone who's a member of our family, who she says she loves and respects, made more of a difference. And if I had, on my own, gotten up and stormed out of the house, I don't think I would have helped, it would have hurt more. And I think it would have been arrogant of me. If [my husband] had just said, "I cannot sit at the table with this woman," I would have left, if that was what he wanted. But it was like he took it with a certain grace and sense of humor, and I think I had an obligation to do the same thing. And I don't think she says stuff like that anymore [laughs].

Referring to an incident of individual racism when a person of color, her husband, was present, Kendra explained why she did not take the more blatant response of walking out. Having realized that her stepmother was well aware of, and regretful of, the racist comment, as well as knowing that her husband wanted to avoid making a scene, Kendra chose her response accordingly. She used the power of eye contact, and then corrected her mother's attempt to avoid responsibility for her own actions. Her mother seemed sufficiently remorseful, and her husband seemed satisfied with the outcome, so she deemed a harsher response unnecessary. She suggested that white antiracists go through a similar process, if possible, when selecting their action strategies. This would allow whites to monitor whether or not they were taking the privileged tendency to overreact.

Like Kendra, Mike is a PI member, and he also talked about keeping his responses to individual racism in check by consulting people of color. Developing "authentic relationships" with people of color for reasons of accountability is a tenet of the PI Undoing Racism workshops for whites, and Mike referred to this tenet when he explained how it can also keep one's tendency to underreact to racism in check:

> I think the challenge for me is constantly examining why I don't say something—am I being strategic, or was I afraid? And it's hard to be honest with yourself, and I think that's another part where having authentic relationships with people of color that are keeping you accountable see it from a different perspective, and sometimes when I'm interpreting it as, "I was just trying to—you know, I don't wanna turn 'em off, I have a plan, I'm gonna meet with them for coffee next week"—so you know, it's like, bullshit! You just, you kept your mouth shut, and you let an opportunity go, that kind of thing. I mean, that's not always the case, and I think that's the challenge to try to develop that awareness with yourself [of] how are you being strategic and why. 'Cause I came from the same [laughs] background—just kept my mouth shut for way too long.

Mike's comments underscore a dialectical tension of white privilege—it means white antiracists have the luxury of going too far, as well as the privilege of not having to go far enough. While Kendra discussed how whites can err too far to the left end of the continuum (table 4.1), Mike pointed out how they can err too far to the right.

This striving to stay to the middle of the continuum—not too far to either end—was captured by Nancy. Here she described walking this fine line between not saying anything and saying too much:

> I think of how many times I hear people who say, "If you're not directly involved in this, don't say anything," or who say, "Oh, I wanted to say something but none of the black students said anything." [Me: You're talking about white people now?] White people, yeah. Or even African Americans who say, "You don't have a right to speak about this issue because you're white." And while I respect the fact that I have to hang back and let people of color say what they have to say and let them speak for themselves, I have a responsibility to speak for myself as a white person who takes responsibility for the fact that racism is our system, we invented it, we benefit from it. And I think that in the best-humored way, we have to confront other white people. . . . [On the other hand,] we kind of take over so much, white people tend to privilege our own voice—step forward too fast, speak too much, control too much. . . . We speak first, we speak longest, we take the floor—it's just a part of privilege I think. . . . And when someone of color wants to speak to an issue of race, we often forget to just relinquish the floor, to step back and to let them speak and to listen and to hold our peace. . . . I know that sounds like a contradiction from what I just said that racism is my thing and it's my responsibility to speak about it. [Me: No, no.] That doesn't mean I need to speak first or most often or longest though.

The theme that emerges from many of the white antiracists here is the struggle to find a balance between one's responsibility as a white person to confront acts of racism and one's subconscious sense of power and privilege over people of color when reacting to the event. When whites are not at home wishing they had said something, people of color might be at home wishing they had been able to get a word in edgewise when that incident of racism had occurred.

These respondents collectively make the point that white *options* for responding to individual racism are very different from those available to people of color—namely, there is a larger variety of socially acceptable responses that white antiracists can practice without as much risk of stigma. Further evidence of this position of privileged resistance is the fact that none of them mentioned being limited by the "second eye" that Feagin's black respondents described—they did not talk about having to consider whether or not they were *sure* something was racist, leaving them more time and energy to consider an effective action strategy. Methods for interrupting individual white racism often did involve a strategy of considering what is the most effective action, given the situation. White antiracists observed that whites can sometimes be too confrontational or not confrontational enough, both strategies resulting in ineffective action. Thus, privileged resistance is described as both a blessing and a burden, a challenging fine line to walk.

MEDIATING PRIVILEGED RESISTANCE: THE FRAME OF MAINTAINING RELATIONSHIPS

How does one know when she or he has done too much or not done enough? How does one know when to come on stronger or to just back off? PI members in particular suggested building "authentic relationships" with people of color who would "hold them accountable," or give white antiracists advice on what would be the most effective or beneficial strategy for ending the racism they encounter. Chapter 6 will give more attention to the notable emotional supports that the PI organization provides white antiracists, but one concept from that discussion worth noting here is the idea of "maintaining relationships." In the PI Undoing Racism workshop, whites learn that they too have cultural behavior (just like "other" cultural communities) that is characterized by a tendency to regard relationships as "disposable." That is, whites are less likely to see other whites as brothers and sisters, and to work to maintain those connections in spite of ideological differences. This becomes relevant to our discussion of privileged resistance because, within this framework, whites would be more likely to confront, without much thought or concern, a racist comment in a way that might destroy their relationship with the person who made the comment. Following a model which seeks to emulate the greater cohesiveness of communities of color, PI challenges whites to "maintain relationships" with other whites. Otherwise, they lose their opportunity to "plant seeds" or usher in antiracist change in these individuals' lives. So PI members were particularly articulate about how the desire to "maintain relationships" factored into their strategies for confronting everyday racism. Take this example from PI member Henry on how he dealt with a coworker:

> Another instance was the training, the last one I was talking about, with my colleague. I was very angry with him and personally had a hard time with him. . . . A couple of the colleagues reminded me that it was the best thing I could do for antiracism to maintain my relationship with him, which I wanted to do. And also, to get over my anger with him, and to listen to him, I was to go be a pastor for him. And so I did. I went and listened. He tried to get me to collude with him several times, and I did not do that. But I did actively seek to maintain my relationship with him, in a supportive way.

Although respondents, regardless of organizational affiliation, spoke about not "flying off the handle" and strategizing responses, PI members used this vocabulary of "maintaining relationships," and they were particularly conscious of how this contributed to a larger process of movement. This gives us insight into why it is only PI members whose names appear at the far right end of the continuum, and no PI members appear on the far left. A neutral initial response that is part of a long term plan (Type 4) clearly reflects this principle of maintaining relationships, and a direct angry confrontation (Type 1) is the most incompatible with it. Thus, organizations are important influences even when antiracists are acting as individuals. While all white antiracists are dealing with the dynamics of privileged resistance, PI members (because of their organizational frame, learned in the training) are especially well equipped to mediate its deleterious effects on the potential for antiracist change.

NO "KNEE-JERK" LIBERALS HERE

Conservative author Dinesh D'Souza (1995) gave voice to what many white Americans were secretly (and not so secretly) thinking when he argued that liberals were quick to cry racism at anything and everything so they could keep their jobs in the "civil rights profession." While D'Souza portrays people of color (particularly blacks) as eager to blame their problems on whites, he regards white antiracists as no more credible since their livelihood depends on pointing out as much racism as they possibly can. Here the image of a "knee-jerk" liberal comes to mind—someone who categorically expresses outrage at anything remotely resembling injustice without giving it much thought. Yet my study reveals that white antiracists are hardly reacting without thinking. Indeed, confronting everyday racism involves using careful strategies that sometimes can even mean saying nothing at all. But if they are saying nothing, it does not mean that they think racism has not occurred. (D'Souza's argument is that if we thought hard enough, we would realize that whites are not being racist at all; they are actually practicing justifiable "rational discrimination"!) While acknowledging the act as a clear manifestation of racism, these white antiracists who respond with initial silence actually may be postponing taking a stand until they can position themselves for greater effectiveness.

But conservatives are not the only ones who stereotype antiracists as reactionary. Even white liberals who find themselves sympathetic to antiracist ideology tend to regard practicing antiracism as a surefire way to alienate others. Citing her own research as well as van Dijk's (1987), Essed (1991) notes that whites "generally fail to take a stand against racism" (276) and this is often "for fear of causing trouble" (277). There are many whites out there who might applaud the efforts of other whites who are antiracist, but perhaps see it as a confrontational lifestyle that they cannot participate in themselves. The heartening contribution that my study offers, particularly to these whites, is the insight that white antiracists actually strive *not* to alienate others by their actions. This is not to say that white antiracists do not at times face repercussions for their actions. Indeed, whites challenging institutional racism have risked their jobs and even their lives, as we shall see in the following chapter. Interrupting everyday racism, or convincing whites to reevaluate their actions, however, does not have to mean yelling at all people for everything they do. Those who shy away from being antiracists because they do not want to be "in your face" all the time are truly missing what antiracism is all about. There is room for even the most shy and soft-spoken white person in the antiracism movement, and in some situations, these might even be the most effective of them all.

This work on finding the most effective strategy given the situation has a very important component for whites, though. That is, the strategy is put together within the context of an understanding of what being white means. Just as people of color in Feagin's (1991) and Essed's (1991) studies were aware that whites would perceive them as biased and overreactive, white antiracists are aware that they are taken as more believable by other whites. Thus, whites have the ability to engage in *privileged resistance*; as compared to people of color, they are less likely to suffer repercussions and social stigma for speaking out about racism. Privileged resistance is evident in many other forms of anti-oppression activism, which makes this concept so important to bring to the forefront of antiracist research. While many activists know this, it has not been systematically named as a major component of antiracist action. What this means is that, relative to blacks, whites spend less time and energy considering whether or not something is really racist (no "second eye"), freeing them to focus more on action itself.

Privileged resistance came alive to me long before I had a name for it and even before I began to study the concepts of racism and privilege in an academic setting. I was a college freshman and the Rodney King beating had just recently been made public. For some reason, my campus had a public showing of Spike Lee's movie *Do the Right Thing* around this time, and student discussion was encouraged after the screening. Predictable racial cleavages emerged during the discussion, with black students talking about police mistreatment and white students talking about how difficult it was to be a police officer and to have to defend oneself when necessary. Timidly I raised my hand and said I had been pulled over by police officers in "routine" traffic stops before and that I had also been in the car with a young African American man when he was stopped by police. In the latter case, I witnessed a completely different "routine," in which my black companion had to place his hands in his lap and was not allowed to reach for his license and registration, lest he be reaching for a gun. While I was saying nothing that the black students in the room had not previously stated or experienced, a funny thing happened in that room. I felt like I was actually getting through to the whites who were initially skeptical that racism existed.[2] And I had not done anything differently than my fellow students of color except to appear "white" while they did not. It was at this point that I felt like I had a gift (through no hard work of my own but simply by way of our racist social arrangements) and that I had a responsibility to use this gift. It was not until I begun my dissertation research several years later that my respondents began to teach me about the challenges inherent in this "gift" of privileged resistance that white antiracists have.

Specifically, these respondents collectively assert that this privileged position unfortunately holds the potential for two pitfalls: (1) one becomes so arrogant and confrontational that effective change is thwarted, or (2) one uses "strategy" as a smokescreen for fear and does not confront racism at all. Although they may not face the accusations of bias and hypersensitivity that people of color do, white antiracists face a different set of considerations they take before acting. In speaking out, are they inadvertently using their voice to silence nonwhite voices of opposition (too far to left side of continuum)? In not speaking out, are they being complacent about racism because they are white and thereby less invested in antiracist change (too far to right side of continuum)? The quotations presented in this chapter may suggest that the respondents here have achieved a perfect balance for themselves between these two extremes. Yet in truth, their comments come from a place of having erred too far to one extreme or the other in their own experiences. At the time of his interview, Mike was focusing on the complacency aspect because he had previously "kept [his] mouth shut for way too long." At the time of their interviews, Nancy and Mac both were working on toning down their approaches because they felt they had been too hot-headed in the past with their actions. The respondents generally presented themselves as works in progress, aspiring to incorporate responsible privileged resistance in their lives.

One way some respondents (particularly PI members) sought to evaluate their progress was through the feedback of people of color. The challenge of negotiating the double-edged sword of privileged resistance certainly could be better met by the process of "accountability" that PI advocates. Accountability to people of color is an important part of white antiracism, according to PI. While this is significant, it becomes difficult in an all-white context. Kendra was married to a person of color, but not all white antiracists are married interracially. PI members also live in a racially diverse urban area, which again is not a unanimous white experience. Yet even within racially diverse communities, as ARA organizer Mac notes, culturally different organizing styles may result in predominantly white antiracist groups. In the absence of accountability networks, then, it is important for white antiracists to keep in mind these two pitfalls of privileged resistance to keep themselves in check.

Another contribution that PI members make to the discussion of confronting everyday racism is the concept of "maintaining relationships." In one of his campaign speeches about race, white Democratic hopeful Bill Bradley spoke about his "Aunt Bub"—a woman who had been like a second mother to him but from whom he distanced himself during his adult life because of her racist comments. Perhaps many white antiracists have their own "Aunt Bub" with whom they have found it difficult to maintain a relationship. One might expect the good white antiracist to sever all connections with "Aunt Bub" and any other friend or acquaintance who makes racist statements or actions. Yet here we find the opposite. Actually, maintaining a relationship with "Aunt Bub" is, in Henry's words, "the best thing I could do for antiracism."

Far from knee-jerk reactors who kick all those who are not "politically correct" out of their lives, PI members are especially vigilant about resisting the temptation to shut out people who do not agree with them. White PI members even have European Dissent meetings where they can vent their frustrations and receive encouragement from other whites when the going gets tough with "Aunt Bub." (See chapter 6 for more on emotional support systems.) Thus, while working toward effective action strategies was common among all white antiracists, maintaining relationships with other whites, and developing relationships of accountability with people of color, were strengths unique to the PI organization. Yet they are strategies all white antiracists can learn from. These strategies speak to the concern, shared across the organizational and nonorganizational activists, of taking a stand that is most effective but neither unprincipled nor undisciplined. This effectiveness is best attained by staying towards the middle of the continuum presented in table 4.1—that is, a careful balance between coming on too strong and not being strong enough. Effectiveness is key, and one way of determining an antiracist's effectiveness is certainly examining the degree to which her/his actions impact institutional change. So we now turn to these whites' institutionally directed actions.

NOTES

1. This is the "white bonding" Paul referenced in the opening quote to this chapter.

2. This must have been beginner's luck, because as an instructor, it typically has taken much more work than this for me to reach a majority of my white students in terms of accepting the facts about racism.

5

FIGHTING THE POWER— CHALLENGING INSTITUTIONAL RACISM

Well, I think everyone, almost everyone relates to some institution or another, whether it's a university, a church, a club, a workplace, and [I would tell antiracists] just really to use that connection in a way that at least brings awareness of racist practices that the institution is perpetuating. And it's sometimes risky. Everyone I assume runs some risks in doing this, because institutions are generally more powerful than the individuals that belong to them. If you're lucky, you don't get hurt.

It may seem scary enough to have to confront individual racist speech and actions, but to some the idea of confronting racism at the institutional level can seem even more overwhelming. Yet as Chester points out above, institutions are not at all removed from our everyday experience. Indeed, all of us as individuals hold institutions together. This means institutional racism is a reasonable target for antiracists; it is not out of reach. Moreover, several scholars of race relations (e.g., Carmichael and Hamilton 1965; Bonilla-Silva 1997; Feagin 2000) have made it clear that as long as we conceptualize racism as merely an issue of personal prejudice, rather than as embedded in social structural arrangements, all antiracist efforts will be futile since they will only be addressing a small part of the overall problem. Racism is part of the everyday routine of the institutions we find ourselves in, and although challenging these sites of racism may be a more risky endeavor than focusing on personal behaviors, it is a necessary task of antiracism to do so.

Within institutions, overt racism may occur, but more likely in today's society are the covert practices which appear as business-as-usual. In his article, "Rethinking Racism: Toward a Structural Interpretation," Eduardo Bonilla-Silva (1997) argued that racism is simply the "normal outcome" of a racialized society. He pointed out that modern racist practices "(1) are increasingly covert, (2) are embedded in normal operations of institutions, (3) avoid direct racial terminology, and (4) are invisible to most whites" (Bonilla-Silva 1997, 476). Seemingly meritocratic admissions policies at a school, for example, are an example of the everyday way in which racism is carried on institutionally, especially when those policies systematically exclude nonwhites. Yet these kinds of policies (e.g., requiring a certain score on an "objective" standardized test) usually are not written with any mention of race. This kind of racism is quite different than overt comments like "let's eat like the white folks" or "black people are lazy" as discussed in the previous chapter, where race is explicitly invoked by the perpetrator. In the case of institutional racism, not only is race likely not to be mentioned, but there may not even be a "perpetrator" to speak of *per se*. Thus, we can expect that white antiracist methods for confronting institutional racism will be quite different than the individual strategies previously discussed. Moreover, organizational frames will continue to have an effect on the extent to which such racism is even targeted by white antiracists.

ACTIVATING INSTITUTIONAL POWER

Obviously racism in institutional settings is most noticeable when it is overt. Sometimes, participants in institutional racism can be overt behind the scenes, yet cover up their prejudices when presenting their proposals publicly. In these cases, white antiracists responded by drawing direct attention to the racial implications of the situation, even when communities first turned a blind eye to the issue. In Nancy's case, a white mother of an African American child, white parents unknowingly exposed to her their prejudiced motivations for wanting to exclude students of color from the gifted program to which her daughter had applied.

> The first night that I went to the parents' meeting . . . the parents were all working on how to get these colored kids out of the program—that was their expression, "the colored kids"—because they knew that they weren't qualified, that they weren't smart, that they would bring down the moral level of the class, and they were talking to me as if I was one of them. . . . And [they assumed] I would agree with them. . . . [once the meeting officially started] I said, "I think we have a real issue here that we need to talk about, which is what are the children in the program now being told about the new children that are in the program now, and I'm very worried about that." . . . And the teacher was like, "Oh, there are no problems about that," and one of the parents actually had the guts to say, "We understand these children don't have the same test scores, that they're not as bright, that they come from troubled homes." Luckily she spoke it out and people were able to talk about it. . . . I know they never felt comfortable with me again and I never felt comfortable with them again, but I think the kids' life was better after that. Parents agreed that they wouldn't talk to them about this issue. You know they talked about it somehow, but it was better.

Nancy's method of confronting the systematic exclusion and devaluation of students of color was to address it head-on. Notably, the teacher was initially in denial about the racial motivation of the problem.

Similarly, Amy faced whites who also tried to mask the racial motivation of their criticisms, except in Amy's case it was her fellow students who were trying to exclude a black professor by complaining about his teaching. Like Nancy, she was also privy to the conversation because as a white person she was assumed to share their sentiments.

> They don't realize there might be somebody in the room that doesn't agree with them, because everybody's white, so of course we all agree. . . . Because—I told you this before—about my teacher and how the people in my class are claiming that he's giving us lower grades because he's black and we're not and whatever! And it has nothing to do with the fact that we all suck. [laughs] So that's like that. And I called the department and told the—[me: You did?] chair. Yeah. I called the department and told the chair that that was going around and that I

thought he should be careful about people's criticisms because they were racially motivated.

While Nancy appealed to the teacher (an authority) in order to deal with the parents, Amy also notified an authority figure—in this case the department chair—to alert them of the racial motivations of individuals. In both cases, the "complainers" are taking advantage of their white privilege within the institution, which dictates that their concerns will likely be validated without question. The complainers expect to use their powers of exclusion without mentioning race, but the white antiracists bring it to the attention of the authorities that unstated racial prejudices lurk behind their statements.

While Nancy and Amy both seemed satisfied with the outcomes of their actions, they also were appealing to authorities who did not have to be in a position to feel "accused" of racism themselves. If the authorities themselves are involved with the racism, or stand to feel attacked if it is brought to their attention, then the white antiracist trying to challenge the racism faces the formidable task of navigating through that defensiveness. Dorothy is one who undertook such a challenge in a work-related situation:

I was working on a research project . . . it just was so clear in the office that the black interviewers, even the supervisor—there was nothing illegal but they were not being treated with respect, it was like a daily invalidation. And I looked at it for awhile. First of all I had a white supervisor, and he was really tight with another white interviewer who'd been there for a long time, and they tried to bring me into their circle. And so I sat down with him alone and pointed out what I saw was happening . . . And I just let them know that I didn't want to be a part of it . . . this other interviewer sort of had easy access to his office all the time, and that was sort of what was being offered to me. And then I also gave Peggy McIntosh's article [on white privilege] to the overall project director. And I suggested well maybe she could hand it out to everyone. . . . She didn't do it and she didn't want to talk about it [laughs] and then the other white interviewer, I gave her that article, or tried to give it to her, and she kind of just moved her whole hand away! And said, "Oh, you think I'm racist." And you know then I tried to explain that in a society where all the institutions were put together during slavery and have been tinkered with but basically they were there for the benefit of whites and whether you want to be or not yeah, we're all racist, you and I both.

Dorothy also faced the challenge of critiquing a less overt, business-as-usual situation. Whites being nice to other whites, cleaving to those with whom they feel most comfortable, are usually not contemplating how they might be excluding others, and most likely see themselves as nice, friendly human beings. Because most whites do define racism in their own minds as overt and prejudicially motivated actions, they are likely to respond in shock when confronted with something like this. This defensiveness exhibited by someone who sees herself as a genuinely good person is evident in the response, "Oh, you think I'm a racist." Dorothy's answer to the defensive response was to redefine racism in a way that was everyday and systemic, and she included herself in the definition. Dorothy admitted that not much was done in response to her initial broaching of the topic, but she remained hopeful that she planted some seeds of thinking differently in her coworkers.

Other white antiracists who hold positions of power themselves are able to use that power to usher in antiracist change, and more likely to be successful at it. Chester, being a Harvard graduate, was conscious of being able to use his position to take stands on certain issues:

> [There are a] couple of things I occasionally have going with my alma mater, Harvard University. Trying to get them to divest in the mid-80s from South Africa, I headed a group called Harvard-Radcliffe Alumni Against Apartheid. Just recently I got some mailing from the alumni office about a spring alumni trip to the antebellum South which included a stop in Charleston and I was trying to make a big issue of the fact that the NAACP and others have called for a boycott of South Carolina until they remove the confederate flag from the statehouse. So [I am] constantly trying to raise awareness and use institutional leverage.

Another relatively prestigious white antiracist, Bob, who is the CEO of a grocery store chain, has every employee go through extensive diversity training, and tries to diversify his work force even in his predominantly white area of the country.

> Our vice president of human resources, is a person of color, he's been with us about two years now. It took us a whole year and a half to find

him, but I had the support of my officers that it would be a person of color. We just refused to settle for anything less, and we're just glad we did; we have an outstanding individual. . . . Because of our position, and because we worked hard within our company to diversify, we have many, many, many more people of color training with us, because it's quite simple, they like to train where they see their own kind, people like them.

Bob also gives regular invited talks in his community on the reality of racism in contemporary America and even has a research institute on racism at a local university named after him. Bob certainly has the power to make racism an important issue to address within his work environment if he so chooses, maximizing the probability of his success.

Obviously not everyone is fortunate enough to be a CEO, but the key to institutional antiracism is simply to start from wherever one finds oneself. Susan made the point that anyone, regardless of the person's job or position, can effect institutional change:

It's just one person at a time beginning to devote more and more of their life energy to this work, so that it becomes less and less of "oh, it's something I do on the weekends and the evenings" and more of "this is what I do for my work"—not necessarily making money off it, but like, "I'm a teacher so this is how I do it," or "I cut hair, so this is how I do it," kind of thing.

Supporting a conceptualization of racism that posits it as embedded in everyday normal routine, Susan emphasized that one can use one's position in any institution to do antiracism. For instance, Jack is not exactly a CEO, but he is the minister of a church, and here is how he activated his institutional power in an antiracist way:

About three years ago we started studying . . . our own congregation— what did we do that was racist in the church, that kept people of African American heritage from not wanting to be with us. Because we only have a few black members. And that was despite—we advertised, from the day I arrived, and maybe it was happening before, we advertised in the local black newspaper, we had connections to that black church, we would go to all the rallies and the MLK day celebrations, and it didn't have any effect. . . . We have gone through a number of training programs, administered and bringing trained professionals in to help us look at what we might do to exclude African Americans, culturally and otherwise. . . . And in the last couple of years we've done some special study groups for the whole congregation on antiracism. What is it and why do we need it? Some of the members of the congregation are pretty much resistant. They say, "Well, I'm not prejudiced" and what's the point of us having to be antiracist if you're against prejudice, that's not enough. And we try and say, well it's the difference between a state of mind and a state of action.

Jack's experience demonstrated that even when the suggestion to institutionalize antiracism comes "from above," there can still be the same kind of defensive resistance that Dorothy faced from her superiors at the research job. In both cases, those who are resistant define racism as prejudice rather than as the normal outcome of society. Again, it becomes the task of the antiracist to move people to understanding a different conceptualization of racism, one that is embedded in everyday social relations of which all whites are a part.

PI member Kendra, while not the head of a company or a church, did have some power relative to her students, being a Sunday School teacher, and was able to incorporate this kind of re-definition of racism into the curriculum. Much like Dorothy did with her coworkers, Kendra drew her students to an understanding of the systemic nature of racism:

I was teaching a Sunday school class to ten-year-olds last week and they said to me, "Everyone's a racist, everyone's a little bit racist." And I said, "No, everyone's *not* a little bit racist. Everyone has some racial prejudice, because of racism. But really, not everybody is a racist." I said, "Racism is something that is when the whole society is set up for one group." I said, "Which [group] is this?" and they could *tell me* that it was white people. . . . *They know* that society is set up by and for white people, they can see it in their experience. And so we talked about some of those things. We talked about who it is that runs the government, who it is that owns most of the banks, who it is that runs the schools, and who it is that makes up standardized tests, and we talked about testing and things like that—things that are in their experience—and they *can* understand the difference, that it is white people who've been given power in this nation. And I think sometimes we think that be-

cause we weren't taught these things when we were ten years old, that
we can't teach them to our kids. And I just think we can!

At least within her classroom, Kendra has the power to make racism an issue, posing a challenge to the predominant elementary
school curriculum which rarely focuses on race except in a "cele-
brating diversity" type of way that does not address structural arrangements of inequality. In opening these students' eyes to these
realities at such a young age, one can only hope that once they
reach adulthood and are in positions of power themselves, they
will be less likely to react with the kind of defensiveness that antiracists like Dorothy and Jack came up against.

Yet in Kendra's case, all we have is "hope." Being a CEO and
being able to implement a concrete hiring plan, stopping at nothing until it succeeds, is quite different from "planting seeds" and
hoping they will blossom. Even Jack, who had power over determining the direction of his congregation, was not in a position to
hire individuals. Making a church, whose membership is voluntary, more diverse is quite different from diversifying a work force.
The degree of power, and the type of power, one occupies within
an institution clearly affects the extent to which immediate antiracist change can be activated by these whites. Often, when one's
power in an institution is not absolute, institutional antiracism
must be conceptualized as an ongoing process, for which results
are not immediately tangible.

Susan's experience at her martial arts school demonstrates this
quest for institutional change as a continual long term process. She
explained:

> I train in martial arts, and there's a women's school I go to here called
> [school name]. When I got there a couple years ago, I basically asked
> the question, why is it so white? [laughter] There were a couple women
> of color, who I wouldn't see very often. And especially for a martial arts
> school, where that comes out of, definitely not out of white America. It
> turned out that the head sansei was saying . . . this is something that's
> come up over the years and we just have to keep talking about it. So she
> got involved in these [antiracist] trainings that we've been doing, and
> there's a couple other people who have taken some of the leadership
> roles in . . . the school and having a conversation, and continuing to
> analyze what it is we're doing and how [it excludes people of color.]

Although she did not describe being met with the resistance that Jack was, Susan has in common with Jack the task of challenging the whiteness of organizations which people join on a voluntary basis. This means that the process is likely to be longer than that of someone who is the position to offer people paying jobs. However, the process was begun by engaging in self-analysis on the part of these institutions, and by making a commitment to restructure in antiracist ways. The results may not be immediate, so white anti-racists cannot always evaluate their effectiveness based on end re-sults. Instead, they envision long-term plans that will bear fruit down the road. They should be diligently working on that plan, though, and not just sitting back and hoping for the best, if they expect those changes to emerge.

Angela, another white mother of a black child, also witnessed racism in other white parents' responses to elementary school poli-cies. In Angela's case, the discussion centered around the city's efforts to integrate the schools:

At my son's school, I was sitting on the wall waiting for dismissal with a couple other white moms, and another white woman who was a mom came up to the group and [said], "I think we're compromising our stan-dards by some of the kids in this school." You can imagine she was saying . . . she really just assumed that the next thing out of my mouth was gonna be an addition to what she said. . . . [I responded:] "I actually don't agree with that" and she was so startled! I said, " I see it quite differently. Are you interested in knowing how I see it?" and of course she said yes. [laughs] I mean she felt socially obligated to say yes at this point [laughs] and then I just sort of started in very real language, not in a lot of political rhetoric, what my experience was in terms of some issues she was talking about, and what my perspective was. And I don't know how she dealt with it or took it because I think at that point probably the kids were coming out or whatever. But afterwards, I thought about it a whole lot. And what it did for me was make me really see that if there's any hope for maintaining any kind of equity in the public schools right now, it's that we've got to be reaching people like them. And so I've sort of rechanneled some of the outside of work activist work that I'm doing focused specifically on my son's school right now because I can't take on the bigger system but there are things I can do within the school. . . . I'll spend this whole year, if not a year and a half, really simply making relationships and just building some credibility with people as sort of a long-term strategy.

Although Angela is not in a position to implement antiracist training for the parents, her strategy, much like those discussed in the
previous chapter, is to foster relationships with individuals she
hopes to educate on the issue. Only this time the strategy is not just
one of personal transformation. It is about marshalling the public
support needed to keep antiracist policies from being repealed. She
mentioned not being able to "take on the bigger system" right now
as a reason for focusing on the individual school setting. She acknowledged that it would be at least a couple of years before she
could even expect to see results of her efforts. As a solitary parent,
rather than a school board or city council member, options for institutional antiracism again are not those which would produce
immediate results. Again we see how crucial the type and degree
of power of the white antiracist is in determining how one can
challenge institutional racism.

OCCUPATIONAL HAZARDS

Because white antiracists seldom hold ultimate power in institutions, there is always the possibility that those above them will
really not appreciate their antiracist efforts. We have already seen
how those who challenge institutional racism can be met with in-
dignation and defensiveness. Yet sometimes the consequences for
challenging institutional racism are more severe than uncomfortable conversations. Ostracism, loss of jobs, and even death threats
were part of the experiences of white antiracists who fought institutional power. On professional ostracism, Mark recalled a time
when, as members of the taxi drivers' union, he and others "took
the heat" for taking an antiracist position.

> There were periods of time when cab driving was a very dangerous
> occupation in [city name]. In any particular year, 7 or 8, 9, 10, 11 cab
> drivers would be murdered because someone would have tried to hold
> them up, and for one reason or another it would have led to violence
> and they would have been shot. And these were also always kind of
> wrenching kinds of stories. And one of the consequences of that was
> that there was a widespread conviction on the part of white cab drivers
> that they should *not* pick up black people because those were the ones
> who were going to either be more likely to rip them off or to kill them,

or to bring them to a neighborhood where that would be more likely to happen subsequently. And so, one of the issues that we had to confront was whether we would be unequivocally in favor of every cab driver picking up every person who wanted a fare. . . . [We were] forthright about saying that, in fact, people had an unqualified right to get a cab when they wanted to, and that's what we should do. And we took considerable heat for that.

The union took the risk of losing some of its power if enough members were disgruntled or displeased with the position. Yet here the disapproval came laterally rather than from superiors. It is when antiracist challenges to the status quo bring disapproval from superiors that the real occupational hazards begin, especially when the white antiracist acts in isolation, rather than in solidarity with other coworkers as in Mark's example.

White antiracists have, in fact, lost their jobs when doing acts of institutional antiracism in isolation. David, now a PI member and organizer, recalled one of his actions during the Civil Rights era:

I was teaching school in [town] the first anniversary of Martin Luther King's assassination. . . . And so I took the students to Memphis to be a part of the march, the commemoration march. And it caused great consternation in the school because the parents were fearful of what would happen to the students. And they were right. We got tear gassed, gangs attacked us—white roving mobs. The students had an incredible experience [laughs] but it could have been really nasty. And when I got back to school, the principal let me go, saying that he couldn't afford to keep me around.

There are two different risks incurred in this example. First, participating in a march honoring Martin Luther King in the South in the late 1960s was bound to attract the kind of white physical violence that David described. Additionally, though, David returned to find that he had lost his job due to his actions.

During the same era, Harriet's career as a journalist was also met with intolerance by her supervisors. She made it a point to use her position as a writer to research and expose local incidents of racism, and this was usually not appreciated:

The new publisher came in and he was on the Urban League board, and he said we should have more coverage on the black community.

And I got assigned to do it. And so I wrote it like it is. And I quoted black people on the racism that made it necessary to set up programs of one kind or another. And my editors hated me, I mean, they hated me!

In this case, Harriet faced hatred from her supervisors, but in another case, she like David lost her job for being antiracist:

I wrote a story about health care, what the blacks were getting and not getting in [name] County, and I included the fact that the local hospital wasn't serving any black people. Because we also complained to Washington after that happened and they sent somebody in, and the hospital straightened up. But anyway, I got fired. [me: You got fired? For what?] It turned out the publisher was on the hospital board.

Because of her insistence in speaking out about institutional racism and challenging power structures, Harriet actually had to move continually just to be able to find a job: "We got people investigated, and we got the feds in on the hospital, and we got the equal employment man down on the employment office and we got the welfare department investigated. . . . Nobody was going to hire me! We [she and her husband] were well known." Harriet made a conscious choice to continue doing this antiracist reporting even when she knew that by its very nature it could regularly be grounds for dismissal. She would rather relocate than compromise her actions.

Never did anyone I interviewed express regret over having lost a job due to their antiracist activities. Some even regarded such losses as blessings in disguise. Drawing upon yet another example from the 1960s, Chester brought up a teaching job he lost:

I lost a reappointment when I was teaching in the city planning department at Harvard in the late 1960s, but that was more kind of a combination of things of which antiracism work was only one. I [gave] a lot of support for the student strike, of which racial issues were fairly central, [and] the kind of teaching I was doing with students. But I don't consider that to be any great loss actually [laughs] to not have remained there as a teacher.

We might like to think that respect for academic freedom has advanced considerably since the 1960s, yet Nancy related a similar experience that was much more recent. Her experience lends support to the argument that contemporary racism typically does not mention race directly. Instead today's institutions invoke seemingly race-neutral criteria which still result in limiting the advancement of people of color. Nancy recalled:

> Because I took such strong stands about racial issues, in my teaching position [pause] that drove a serious wedge between me and the rest of the faculty, and that I believe seriously impacted my career and my willingness to stay at that institution. . . . [The department] wrote me this letter that no one signed. "Dear Nancy," signed by no one! But it was from the entire faculty tenure and promotion committee, except for the African Americans who weren't tenured. [The letter] said, "We believe that you will never publish things that we accept"—because everything I was doing about race stuff— . . . "We believe that you are a bad fit for this institution." . . . And I had to say, am I going to stay and make a fight of this, or am I going to pack it in? Which was too bad because I love teaching. But I really think it was a blessing in disguise. . . . It was the relationship [I had] with the students of color, it was my stand on those issues, it was always wanting to teach those courses and be involved in those issues, it was replacing half of the white supervisors in the clinic with African American supervisors, when the white supervisors . . . were very popular. But where were we going to find black mentors, for our black and white students? So I think it was those things, and the time that those things took, that really drove a wedge between me and the faculty.

Nancy's efforts at this school clearly attempted to alter racist structural arrangements. At first she was reluctant to tell me the story because she felt, since race was not mentioned directly in the letter, her interpretation would likely be different than that of the school, and they would deny any racial motivations.[1] However, it is evident, especially under the definition of racism we have developed here, that racism was activated in this seemingly race-neutral decision. Nancy's publications which dealt with racial issues were described as unacceptable, and her challenges to the racial status quo in the department no doubt were behind her being a "bad fit" for the institution. Many may feel that racism has improved since the 1960s, yet the only difference between the 1960s examples and this one is how the decision was communicated (without overt racial language). The end result is identical.

It is notable that the most serious consequences for antiracist action in institutional settings are incurred by those who act in isolation. Taxi drivers deciding as a group to stand behind a policy were not systematically fired, but individual teachers are easily ousted for taking a stand. The difference between the risks of acting alone and acting as a group are best illustrated by contrasting two different situations, both of which were protests against racist fraternities. In the first example, Amy and one of her friends were concerned that a fraternity at their university was using the Confederate flag as their symbol. Amy had done some research of her own which revealed that this fraternity had been started as the "academic arm of the KKK," and when she later returned to the library to retrieve the book that stated this fact, Amy found that the page had been ripped from the book. This was one indicator that she was up against power greater than her own. However, she continued to challenge the fraternity, and they flexed their muscles to threaten her.

> We were going to hang signs that said . . . "The Confederate Flag: 400 Years of Oppression or a [frat name] Tradition? You Decide." And we hung them up all over campus one night when everyone was asleep. . . . like an idiot, I wrote, "For more information, contact Amy" [laughs] And I wrote my number on it, right?! And my PO Box, so of course, what do I get? Millions of harassing phone calls, and [frat name]'s telling me they're going to sue me for defamation! And I'm like, well, it's true, it was their symbol! I don't know what they thought they were going to sue me for, but so I had all these people like calling me up, and all these people leaving me notes in my mailbox telling me I was going to die and I started getting death threats and stuff, whatever, people saying they were going to burn a cross and shoot me.

Not only was Amy up against a group larger than she and her one friend, but the group was a fraternity in long-standing good relationship to the university, undoubtedly a source of sizeable alumni contributions. So even as another paying student, she was not likely to receive protection from her university. In fear of these death threats, Amy actually transferred to a different institution to finish her degree.

PI members also challenged a racist fraternity in their area, but this action was done by European Dissent as a group, so individual harassment was not a problem as in Amy's case. This particular fraternity advertised that they were going to celebrate Martin Luther King, Jr.'s, birthday by "having Popeye's chicken, watermelon, and 40s [forty ounce malt liquor]." Because this fraternity had "very prominent historical Americans" as members, including George Bush, Neil Armstrong, and several of their state's governors and representatives, the community turned a blind eye toward their racism, "where boys will be boys was the attitude about it." Again, we see that fraternities can wield a lot of power, especially due to their alumni connections. PI member Lisa recalled how her group responded to this incident. "European Dissent got together with some other groups and we organized a press conference in the name of white people, to come out and say that this is not OK, and that we're not going to stand for this." Not only was Lisa accompanied by her own group, but their organization also joined with other community groups to speak out against the fraternity's racist propaganda. Thus it was impossible for the fraternity to strike out and harass one person. Furthermore, while Amy was a member of the university community to which the fraternity belonged, Lisa and her allies were not part of the institution that supported the fraternity they were protesting, so they did not need its support in any way. In "biting the hand that fed her," Amy could not expect her actions to be backed or defended, so continuing to live in her own environment became unsafe. In contrast, Lisa's immediate living situation was not threatened or affected by her action. There seems to be safety in numbers, and in being at arm's length from the target of your action.

FRAMING INSTITUTIONAL ANTIRACISM

For a large majority of the examples I have presented here, white antiracists have fought systemic racism within institutions that they are affiliated with in some capacity. It is no accident that ARA members are absent from these accounts. Because ARA has framed racism as overt acts of hate and intolerance, such as those of the KKK and police brutality, ARA members are less likely to take activist stands within the institutions in which they live and work. With the exception of ARA organizer Mac, who makes a living as a police misconduct lawyer, ARA members focused on taking stands against bigoted individuals like neo-Nazis. Even Mac's legal activities center around challenging an institution (the police force) of which he is not a member. Although the last account in the previous section describes a protest led by PI members, this was a relatively rare event for white antiracists affiliated with PI. A large majority of the PI members' accounts deal with challenging racism within their own institutions. In fact, the PI Undoing Racism workshop encourages this type of focus. The trainers in the workshop talk about being "gatekeepers," and that people who are gatekeepers in institutions should "exploit the gate"—that is, use their institutional power to create antiracist change. These contrasting frames of ARA and PI, as discussed in earlier chapters, explain why PI members are much more present in this chapter than are ARA members, since here we have defined institutional racism as part of the normal everyday functioning of society, as does PI.

Today's everyday racism is often covert, but as Bonilla-Silva (1997) notes, racism encompasses overt as well as covert practices. ARA is not misguided to focus on overt acts—this is important and necessary work. However, to simply end there misses a large portion of contemporary racism which also occurs in corporate offices, university tenure proceedings, school boards, and the like. Because of ARA's selective race cognizance, members are aware of institutional racism, but are not reflexive about their *own* role or position within those institutionalized arrangements. This is why ARA members do not seem to direct their activism toward organizations of which they are a part. Conversely, PI's frame that posits all whites as racist means that they are often focusing on the subtleties of their own environment, and taking public stands against overt racism such as the fraternity is not often a part of their agenda. Clearly, both of these groups should expand their focus to target both the overt and covert racism in institutions.

Yet a majority of white Americans, whether antiracist or not, already for the most part do not condone overt racism. Although the media does not alert us to how widespread the occurrences of police or neo-Nazi brutality are, at least portrayals for the most part agree that it is wrong and should be stopped. By contrast, a concept of racism that focuses on the subtle, everyday, business-as-usual is largely absent from mainstream media and political discussion. This is why antiracist organizations should be in the forefront of raising awareness on this matter. Not only would institutional racism then be targeted more comprehensively, but whites would be able to visualize more possibilities for antiracist action. Rather than having to search for people with white hoods or shaved heads to protest against, whites could begin in their own churches, schools, and workplaces to make antiracism not just a special event but an everyday way of life.

NOTE

1. Nancy's decision to use her real name in this book heightened these concerns.

SUSTAINING THE PERSONAL STRUGGLES OF WHITE ANTIRACISM

> All of race work is a mine field, and no matter how lightly you step or how carefully you walk or how well you plan your journey, things are going to explode beneath your feet. And when they explode, you're going to lose your leg, or lose an arm. That's the nature of the work. But [like a salamander] once you blow off a leg, you regenerate.

Nancy used the analogy of a salamander, which "regenerates" itself after sustaining injuries, to describe the nature of antiracist work. She expressed both the inevitability of challenges along the way and the necessity of not letting those struggles become debilitating. It is crucial to acknowledge that white antiracists undoubtedly will be bombarded constantly with cultural messages that discourage them from doing this work. Moreover, they will face these challenges from all angles. Other whites in their lives may not be supportive, people of color may be distrustful of them or criticize their actions, and they may even become their own nemeses as internalized racial messages plague their consciousness. It will be the goal of this chapter to explore those challenges which are unique to white antiracists and to analyze the multiple ways in which they cope with the challenges, keeping in mind the influence of organizational framing on these factors.

We have already seen that for whites becoming antiracist requires an ideological shift where they begin to see issues of race differently than the majority of whites. However, this process is not only a cognitive one but an emotional-psychological one as well. Beverly Daniel Tatum, author of the book *Why Are All the Black Kids Sitting Together in the Cafeteria?* (1997), is a black psychologist who popularized the theory of racial identity development. In this influential book, Tatum drew upon the work of Helms (1990), who is the original author of the six stages of racial identity development. These stages apply to blacks and whites. For whites, the stages outline the journey to a secure antiracist identity, which admittedly a minority of whites ever actually achieve. Because the stages work from the assumption of the rarity of white antiracists, they are useful in understanding whites' emotional challenges on the journey to an antiracist identity, but do little to address the challenges they face once there. Nevertheless, it will be useful to briefly outline the stages here.

The stages in order are Contact, Disintegration, Reintegration, Pseudo-Independence, Immersion, and Autonomy. The first three represent those of a racist or nonracist, and it is the last three that typify the journey toward antiracism.[1] Those in the first stage (Contact) do not have much awareness of racism, see themselves as "normal" (Tatum 1994, 464), and often experience feelings of fear and of "discomfort with the unfamiliar" (Jones and Carter 1996, 9). Those in the second stage (Disintegration) start to learn about racism yet grapple with the "societal pressure not to notice, or at least not speak up" (Tatum 1994, 467). They may feel guilty, ashamed, or angry and use denial or withdrawal to deal with these feelings. The despair of "there's nothing I can do" is one example of this withdrawal, and skepticism about evidence of racism is one example of how whites manifest denial. In the third stage (Reintegration), whites deal with this fear and anger by blaming the victim. Tatum gives the example of one of her students saying "it's not my fault that I'm white" and expressing anger at people of color because she feels like she is being "attacked" by them (1992, 15). At this point whites have accepted the evidence about racism but turn it around so that people of color are seen as bringing it on themselves.

While the above three stages are incompatible with antiracism, the next three represent a movement "toward a nonracist white identity" (Jones and Carter 1996, 7). The first of these three stages is Pseudo-Independence. "At this stage, the individual is abandoning beliefs in white superiority, but may still behave in ways that unintentionally perpetuate the system" (Tatum 1992, 16). As with the Disintegration stage, there is still some guilt about being white, but this time it is expressed in a tendency to distance oneself from whiteness by allying oneself with people of color. Racist whites disgust those in this stage, yet they have not examined whiteness deeply enough so that when they develop these interracial relationships they "ignore difference" (Jones and Carter 1996, 16). A search for how one can embrace whiteness without being racist begins with the next stage of "Immersion." Here whites begin to seek out positive white role models and ways of being in the world where they will not have to reject whiteness altogether, and guilt is being replaced by excitement about finding others like oneself. The final stage, of Autonomy, is when one internalizes these positive definitions of oneself, characterized by calmness and security. One has in a sense *become* those "role models" she or he had sought to get to know in the previous stage.

The white antiracists I studied did recall going through some of these stages of guilt, anger, denial, and especially distancing themselves from other whites. In this chapter I will review some of those experiences. It will become evident that indeed being "stuck" in any of these positions does interfere with effective antiracism, and achieving what Helms has labeled as Autonomy would seem to be a necessary precondition for antiracism. Yet the emotional-psychological struggles do not end there. Even Autonomous white antiracists are persistently tested by criticism from both whites and people of color, and the tenacity of their commitment is challenged on many levels. In particular, gaining the respect and trust of people of color, who make up the majority of the national antiracist presence, is crucial to white antiracists' work, and attaining that respect and trust has been an ongoing challenge for many.

According to my research, the two main barriers whites face in establishing that kind of trust are (1) lack of true *empathy* and (2) lack of openness to criticism and willingness to admit mistakes—what one activist of color referred to as *humility*. In regard to the first barrier, many whites with good intentions may unintentionally display *false empathy* toward people of color. False empathy is rooted in making faulty assumptions during antiracist struggles. Richard Delgado, who developed the term, explained,

> False empathy is worse than none at all, worse than indifference. It makes you overconfident, so that you can easily harm the intended beneficiary. You are apt to be paternalistic, thinking you know what the other really wants or needs. You can easily substitute your own goal for his. You visualize what you would want if you were he, when your experiences and needs are radically different. (Delgado 1996, 31)

People of color tend to be distrustful of whites who want to dictate their own antiracist agenda without being truly empathetic to the needs of people of color in the community. This false empathy can evidence itself in a variety of forms, from wanting to "be patient" or move too slowly on an issue to wanting to approach it in a radical way where too much risk would be incurred. One activist of color referred his experiences with white antiracists' false empathy:

> I saw a lot of whites that talked the talk, but never really sort of gave up their white supremacy beliefs, whether conscious or unconscious. And for example when we were pushing a particular agenda, these folks came behind and tried to tell us how to basically organize and how to proceed in the movement. . . . These are the folks, in terms of practical matters were middle-class, settled, nothing would happen to them and still they sort of chastised us because in their estimation we were not radical enough and they wanted us to be more radical. I was like, "Look, this is not a revolution, this is a very restricted struggle here and the conditions are not such to be aspiring for a revolution." . . . I'm talking about socialist folks who claimed to be on our side, but in truth were more interested in telling us how to run the movement.

Even as white antiracists see themselves as being against white supremacy, this account makes the point that they could also unwittingly be participating in white supremacy behavior by dictating an agenda. This becomes a barrier to building multiracial justice movements and a challenge for white antiracists who may be hurt and confused by the distrust that results from their behavior.

The second barrier white antiracists face in gaining the acceptance of people of color is in their lack of humility. This is of course closely related to false empathy since, as Delgado points out, false empathy comes from a place of overconfidence. Part of humility is being open to criticism without becoming defensive and being willing to expose one's vulnerabilities. Of humility, the activist of color quoted above had this to say:

> Humility is something that white people need big time. Because even in these antiracist organizations I have found that many of them develop this notion that I am better than anybody. Some of them develop the belief that they are better than the average white because they're beyond [them] and then some of them believe they're better than us because they understand.

Again, the words "better than" point to a position of superiority or white supremacy that is communicated via refusal to be humble or vulnerable. While the previous example of false empathy during multiracial organizing demonstrated how barriers are erected, the following example of vulnerability shows how white antiracists can successfully establish interracial trust among antiracists. Another activist of color shared this example from a workshop she attended:

> There was a man I admittedly would say all of my categories of rich, white, man, of a privileged background. In the course of [a workshop] he started talking and making himself vulnerable. . . . He talked about the difficulty of how one of his best friends that he hadn't seen in over ten years had come to his house for Christmas and in the course of his stay there began to say some bigoted things and the pain that this man had to go through to ask this man to leave his house. This was somebody that he had grown up with. Him talking about that and sharing it gave me a different view and has allowed me to have some different conversations with white people when I'm talking with them about race issues and for me that was one of the most memorable moments [and] also one of the most positive.

Exposing their own humility and vulnerability is one of the most difficult challenges for white antiracists, even after achieving an Autonomous white racial identity. But we can see from this account that facing this challenge head-on is crucial to overcoming yet another challenge of gaining the trust and respect of people of color.

The personal struggles of white antiracists can thus be understood through a combination of perspectives. First, there is the struggle to achieve an Autonomous racial identity, which includes navigating through the tumultuous waters of one's own prejudice, anger, and guilt about being white and wanting to dissociate from other whites. Next, once one achieves an Autonomous racial identity, there comes the challenge of having to accept criticism, skepticism, and distrust, and exposing one's vulnerabilities in order to earn the trust of others doing antiracist work. Here we will explore how white antiracists negotiate these struggles, paying particular attention to the degree to which different organizational frames equip whites for weathering these trials and tribulations.

STRUGGLING TOWARD AN AUTONOMOUS WHITE RACIAL IDENTITY

Although the first three stages of racial identity development (Contact, Disintegration, Reintegration) are not typical of white antiracists, some of the activists I interviewed did recall struggling through those stages on their way to becoming antiracist. I asked the respondents when they first became aware of racism, which was basically asking them when they emerged from the Contact stage and faced the reality of racism. Their stories attest to the fact that learning about racism is not just a cognitive process, but it is also an emotional process. PI member Henry described his emotional response upon attending his first Undoing Racism workshop:

> I left the first workshop angry, saying "I don't have any privileges that black folks don't have. I see a lot of them who are much better situated financially, professionally, and that sort of stuff than I am." And then I started thinking about it, and talking about it more with other people and then I got it. It took going to some more workshops.

Recall that in the Reintegration stage, the typical emotion is anger directed at people of color. It is a way of redirecting any potential guilt one might feel for being white once one learns about white privilege. Those in the previous stage, Disintegration, focus that discomfort internally by feeling guilty about white privilege. Elizabeth recalled struggling through those feelings "Once you have become aware of these things, there's a white guilt thing. It's like, what do I do with this now that I know these things? And how do I keep from letting it make me feel terrible all the time?" Elizabeth's guilt (Disintegration) and Henry's anger (Reintegration), although fitting into different stages of racial identity development theory, are similar in that they are white reactions to learning about racism which result in inaction. Many whites remain in these stages, doing nothing about racism, and certainly not becoming antiracist.

The challenge for whites is to face the stark realities of racism without letting these common emotional reactions prevent them from doing anything about it. The way they typically do that is by coming to understand racism on a historical and systemic level without excessively blaming themselves for it. Another PI member Pam also reflected on the Undoing Racism workshop and explained her struggle to depersonalize the information she learned so that she could accept it:

> That was tough for me to swallow at the training, that—any white person regardless of where you're coming from—if you're a very prejudiced person, you can't swallow that, that's not going to happen [and] if you're somebody like me, it's still tough to swallow, because I don't wanna believe that of myself. But if you look at the true historical definition of it then yes, I'm a racist. I'm white, I take advantage of the privileges that I have as a white person.

Learning about racism and her own role in it as a white person was "tough to swallow" for Pam, but focusing on the "historical" aspect of it allowed her to get through that difficulty.

Part of becoming aware of racism for whites also means facing their own prejudices, which they have internalized through a lifetime of racist conditioning. Again, the key to not wallowing in guilt when acknowledging these internalized messages is to recognize their societal origins. Bob explained,

> I have to be honest too, every now and then I catch myself, when I come in contact with the first time, or on television a person of color, there's

always still just a little reaction. So I make the statement that it's almost impossible to live in this society and not be racist, in some manner, shape or form. That doesn't mean you're wearing a white sheet on the weekend, or [me: right] but the mere separation alone will cause you to have different thoughts about people who are different.

Most notable is the honesty in this statement, which bespeaks the humility for which we know activists of color have been calling. Also the racial "separation" or segregation which is quite glaring between blacks and whites in the United States is what Bob referenced to explain his "little reaction." In working through emotions, whites who are able to see the societal origins of their prejudices may be more likely to move on to becoming antiracist. Paul was articulate about this process:

Understanding racism . . . in our society is part of the air we breathe, and it's not my fault that I've taken it in and I have it in me, and I'm still aware of a number of prejudices I have around a lot of things. The difference is that now . . . I have a sense of where they're coming from. I have to acknowledge that I grew up in a racist, sexist, homophobic, classist society and I have all that in me. And I can't help it, it's not my fault, but if I know it, I feel I have to act and I have a responsibility to change things.

The difference between whites in Disintegration or Reintegration stages and whites who are antiracist is that recognition of racism is coupled with a "responsibility to change things" rather than a deflection of that responsibility. One has to move out of Contact, Disintegration, and Reintegration stages to become antiracist.

The next three stages (Pseudo-Independence, Immersion, and Autonomy) represent the antiracist journey. In all cases, whites have accepted responsibility for taking action against racism. Yet during Pseudo-Independence, whites are still experiencing some guilt about being white, which they circumvent by avoiding whites altogether. In this case, they are doing antiracist work, but according to Helms, their racial identity is not fully developed. Pseudo-Independence occurs in large part because of the lack of visible white antiracist role models. Whites begin to feel a moral imperative to do something about racism, and they have difficulty reconciling this stance with a white identity. The cultural invisibility of whiteness and antiracism put together is perhaps best illustrated by the comment "she's not really white" that people of color sometimes use affectionately when referring to a white ally. Being white and being antiracist are seen so often as mutually exclusive that it is no wonder that Pseudo-Independence is common among white antiracists. Racial identity development theory says that the key to moving beyond this stage is to learn about other white antiracists (Immersion). After this learning process, one reaches Autonomy, feeling secure doing antiracist work whether surrounded by whites, people of color, or both.

When I started interviewing these white antiracists for my dissertation, I had just moved from one graduate program (and from one state) to another, completely unaware that I was also transitioning from Pseudo-Independence to Immersion as I began the work. For nearly ten years, my social circle was predominantly people of color, from my best friend to my romantic partner to my academic mentors. I would beam with pride when I was told I was "not really white." Yet at my new graduate program, my mentor was a white antiracist, my new best friend was a white antiracist, and I even started dating my first white person. For the first time I formed personal relationships with white people who shared my ideals, and through this research met the numerous white antiracist role models that society had hidden from me for so long. Serendipitously, this project became part of my Immersion process. As they described their experiences moving from Pseudo-Independence to Immersion and then to Autonomy, these white antiracists seemed to foreshadow my own path.

Take PI member Mike, for example, who recalled the emotions of being Pseudo-Independent and what was needed to move beyond it:

> I've seen this as a progression, though. I've seen a lot of white people go through this. They get real disgusted with white culture, because when you become aware of the reality of what has been done by the white collective, it's kind of disgusting. I personally went through a process where there was very few people that I wanted to be around, in my life, and since most of the people in my life were white—outside of my work—most of the real personal relationships I had were with white people. And I just wasn't wanting to be around most of the people that

had been my support system. And that was real disappointing for a long time, it put me in a real difficult place. And that's progressed to the point where I understand that . . . there's work for me to do within the white community.

Not unlike those who moved out of Disintegration and Reintegration stages, Mike emerged from Pseudo-Independence by accepting responsibility—but here it is not just the responsibility for fighting racism, but a more specific responsibility to include other whites in that work. Similarly, Nancy viewed herself as recently having made this "progression" as well. An activist since the 1960s, who "was still doing SNCC[2] stuff when all the white people were thrown out of SNCC," she had lived and worshipped in black communities up until just a few years prior to our interview. She explained:

I wanted to be part of the solution. I didn't understand how to be a part of that solution within the white community—at all! Even when Malcolm [X] started saying go back to your own community, I was like, you don't know where I come from! [We laugh together.] You know what I mean? [more laughter] . . . because we knew we couldn't go home, our parents would never speak to us again [nor would] the people in our hometowns. What he really should have said was go to some other town [more laughter] because I sure couldn't go home again! But then on the other hand, I'm showing absolute respect for what he meant by that, so I'm not trying to make light of that . . . I've learned over the years how much I have to do to be willing to come back and work in the white community and work on antiracism with white people. . . . But if I heard myself saying this a few years ago, Eileen, I would have thought I was a nut! . . . And that was the hardest trip I've ever had to make [me: Wow!] was from living very, very comfortably in African American neighborhoods, and living with my friends, and surrounded by predominantly African American culture and stuff, to saying it is my responsibility, if I mean that sincerely, to make this move and work with white people.

Nancy's life story was punctuated by the contrast between her two children, one white son and one black daughter. In the only time during any of the interviews when I became teary eyed, Nancy expressed the deepest regret over not being able to give her white son positive white role models when growing up. She recalled her son's devastation the day he realized he was not black, and he wished he had been adopted like his sister, because that would have meant his white mother had "chosen" him in the same way as his black sister. In a personal way, Nancy finally understood the "responsibility" of doing antiracist work with white people, and realized that surrounding herself solely with African Americans not only averted part of that responsibility, but also shortchanged her own personal relationships. Clearly, then, the movement toward an Autonomous white identity means moving out of Pseudo-Independence and reconnecting with whites in an antiracist way.

This reconnection with whiteness should not be confused with a rejection of blackness. Indeed, activists of color also recognize the necessity of whites getting beyond the Pseudo-Independent stage and reaching out to their "peers." One person of color asserted,

> Oftentimes I find white antiracist workers a bit judging. I think that they set themselves above their white peers. I think that often this marker of antiracism gets worn as a banner that yeah, I'm down with the black people, the colored people, the whatever people. . . . Call your peers to the table! My main quest would be that this is all good and great, but we would get along even better if I saw you sticking your neck out there, calling your own folks to the table. Not in a condescending way, not in a way that says you're better than they are, but really call them to the table to have the discussion.

In using the phrase "I'm down with the black people," she described the typical Pseudo-Independent stance. She reserved her ultimate respect for those white antiracists who were willing to reach out to their "own folks" when doing antiracist work—something that Nancy pointed out was advocated by Malcolm X decades ago. The Immersion stage of reconnection with whiteness, however, is followed by the Autonomous stage, where ultimately one is comfortable doing antiracist work with whites *and* with people of color. According to racial identity development theory, the process should not end with focusing on whites alone. Another activist of color was clear about this kind of progression as well:

> I think that one of the problems of some of the antiracist organizations in the U. S. is that there is still too much focus on white folks. . . .

Although I understand the need to first join souls to share the same vision, I think that quickly they need to turn from that to interracial organizing. . . . The antiracist organization cannot remain white if it is going to be successful. You have to push for larger goals and then in the process, if it is led by a minority, fine. So it cannot be just your sort of antiracist coalition of all whites. That won't fly.

Thus, Immersion is best understood as a transitory process by which one develops self-confidence in whiteness in order to work comfortably and effectively in a multiracial setting (Autonomy). This man of color believes that whites should move "quickly" from Immersion to Autonomy if they desire success in their organizing.

Developmental stage theories may make transitions seem easy on paper, but clearly the emotions expressed throughout this section point to difficult struggles along the way. Whether race-related or not, any psychological challenge in life often is sustained by some network of support. Thus, we turn now to the organizational resources available for this process.

BEYOND PSEUDO-INDEPENDENCE: PI'S MAINTAINING RELATIONSHIPS

In my own and in other white antiracists' experiences, one of the most difficult transitions in the six stages above is the movement out of Pseudo-Independence, described as taking decades to occur in some cases. As we have seen, one barrier to this transition is the lack of visible white antiracist role models. Yet another barrier is the inability for whites to see themselves as members of a racial group. Paul remarked:

First of all, [I should] not [be] wanting to do this to get a pat on the back from people of color, and always knowing that when I walk into a room I'm carrying a lot of baggage with me, and while I've never been taught all my life to think that I'm part of a group, I am part of a group. I have a friend who said when whites can out David Duke we will have come a long distance. . . . I think if we can get whites even to move to that point where they understand that [they are part of a group], then we'll see some progress.

Paul was insightful about the lifetime of socialization which teaches whites to think of themselves in individualistic terms, such that it may not occur to them that they have a responsibility to their "white peers." This contrasts with the experiences of people of color who grow up with much more of a sense of obligation to "their people."

Although Paul was not a PI member, he described a philosophy which is a crucial part of the PI Undoing Racism workshops. In contrast to ARA which frames overt acts of "hate" as the antagonist, PI frames racism as the antagonist—defined as "race prejudice plus power" or a "bias in favor of whites." Because PI's focus is not only on individuals and groups who profess and/or practice hate, but on an entire systemic process, they focus on those who are both on the "giving" and "receiving" ends of racism and how they are affected by it. As such, PI's Undoing Racism workshop covers both Internalized Racial Oppression (IRO) and Internalized Racial Superiority (IRS), which they argue is experienced by people of color and whites, respectively, under the current structure of U. S. racism. Within this framing, white PI members consider the effects of racism on themselves just as seriously as they consider its effects on people of color, making explicit that those respective effects are very different.

One example of this dual-focus framing comes from the PI workshop which, as stated in chapter 1, is necessarily multiracial. Participants are asked to go around the room and say what they like about being white or black, and the trainers place the answers in two different columns depending on the person's race. When the exercise is over, the trainers point out visually how virtually everything on the white side is about power (i.e., "I like that I am represented adequately in history books, that people don't look past me because of my race," etc.) and nearly everything on the black side is about culture (i.e., "I like our music, feeling like a family/sense of unity," etc.). They point out that whites have traded their culture for power (and also mention that "assimilated" blacks sometimes give up their culture for power as well). Then in a later segment of the training, they state that one of the barriers to building a movement across racial lines is whites' sense of individualism and lack of a sense of membership to a larger collective.[3] Thus, PI whites have been warned that their cultural conditioning has taught them to think of themselves individualistically, and that this will be a barrier they need to overcome. So when it came up, they were articulate about recognizing it and naming it in a way that most other antiracists in the sample were not. This allowed them to transition out of Pseudo-Independence much more quickly than non-PI members.

As part of the Undoing Racism workshops, whites are urged to "maintain relationships" with other whites, to not see them as "disposable." This means when white antiracists tire of their white friends or family members who "don't get it" or when they are embarrassed to be associated with whites who have blatant misunderstandings about race (a Pseudo-Independent response,) that they resist the temptation to "bolt" and instead hang in there and keep trying to make change. PI member Kendra explained:

> I think that I lived in a world where everything's too disposable, and antiracism taught me that, for oppressed communities to survive, it has to [sic] not see relationships as disposable. And I think it's sort of like privilege, there's this disposability of everything, and it's pushed me and challenged me around that. Even with my family, there are ways in which my relationships with my family were disposable that they're not anymore. So it's been powerful in that way.

Kendra described Pseudo-Independent behavior, or distancing oneself from other whites, as "sort of like privilege." In other words, whites have the privilege of being more likely to succeed in the world in the absence of group support. Moreover, in Pseudo-Independence, whites are disengaging from the white-controlled institutions where they could be making positive change for people of color. Again, this reinforces the point that people of color are likely to be distrustful of Pseudo-Independent whites.

Clearly, being Pseudo-Independent means alienating other whites, but it also results in alienating people of color since it is an affront to their own experience in fighting oppression. Thus, it behooves white antiracists' standing with whites and with people of color to maintain their relationships with other whites. PI member David delineated this point.

> The [People's] Institute would later talk to me about how important it would be for me to maintain my relationship with my family and thus

model, [or] attempt to model, how other whites must always keep the connection, must not write each other off, must try to keep from being split all the time in the many ways that white folks split themselves and divide themselves from each other. . . . We're socialized to either make us [sic] individuals or to create an identity that was compartmentalized. And the communities of color were all working all collective[ly], culturally rooted, where regardless of the dynamics that might exist, and the stresses and strains and negatives, and positives, that there was a collective reality. And they were saying that whites come in as individuals or as identity-focused or in other ways kind of compartmentalized and that this was a problem, . . . what the [People's] Institute would later call white cultural behavior.

At the Undoing Racism workshop I attended, David's eighty-something-year-old mother sat through the duration of the workshop in which David was a trainer. Apparently her agreement to finally do this was the result of many years of David's work on maintaining a relationship with her.

Although PI's frame of antiracism at the institutional level distances it from the more psychological perspective of racial identity development theory, we see that PI distinctly encourages its white members away from the Pseudo-Independent stage. PI members also have the benefit of their group European Dissent, in which they can process through many of the struggles of antiracism with other whites who understand. Because PI members are given all these specific strategies within the workshop for working through these struggles, it is likely that they will move further and more quickly through the stages of racial identity development and achieve Autonomy than those whites who do not have access to these resources.

POST-AUTONOMY STRUGGLES: FROM FALSE EMPATHY TO HUMILITY

While racial identity development theory is useful in interpreting the processes outlined above, it does little to explain the challenges white antiracists face once they reach Autonomy. The emotions of the Autonomous stage are described as calmness and security, yet being a white antiracist in today's society can hardly be characterized as peaceful. White antiracists will continue to face criticism from other whites as well as from people of color. No matter how well developed their racial identity is or how far along on their antiracist journey they are, white antiracists are likely to be distrusted by people of color. As I have established, one of the biggest barriers to establishing that trust is false empathy. Here I will review some examples of when white antiracists have exhibited false empathy, along with white antiracists' reflections on what has helped them move toward true empathy in their work.

Jason, a young ARA member, displayed an instance of false empathy when he told the following story. Here he described an incident at the Lollapalooza tour (a concert event) where he was "tabling" for his antiracist organization:

> There was a table almost beside us, like two tables over, who were in MTV's Choose or Lose thing, the voter registration drive. There was probably about fifteen to twenty people staffing it, and they were all black people. And when they were setting up, [we asked them] "Oh who are you guys with?" [they said] "MTV's Choose or Lose," and I was like, "Oh that's pretty cool." And one of the people there asked us who we were with, and we said "Anti Racist Action" and I heard a snicker. [laughs] Like that. And my guard just went up, and I was like, "what was that for?" I almost wanted to say to him, "You should be working with us, rather than working for MTV!"

This example is reminiscent of the situation in the opening section of the chapter where an activist of color was told by white antiracists that he was "not radical enough." Notice that Jason's reaction was also coming from a place of defensiveness, having felt he was criticized by a person of color. Although racial identity development theory shows how defenses can be used to deflect responsibility for becoming antiracist, Jason is an antiracist who wants to do the work. Yet until he examines the supremacist origins of some of his thinking, it is likely he may struggle in gaining the respect and trust of antiracists of color.

Like Jason, PI member Rosalind also struggled with her tendency to adopt a paternalistic attitude towards people of color. She was a bit older than Jason and described a maturation process where she was beginning to try and understand why people of color might opt for different methods of antiracism and community organizing than she would have them select.

> I still sort of feel like I'm beating my head against the wall when I try to work with [name of predominantly African American community]. I don't know how much you know about them, but they are unusual about being pretty far along in self-determination and community empowerment in terms of [a] really oppressed community. But I've been very frustrated in the partnership areas. They'll demand that we meet and work together, and then they won't [pause] they won't do it! And I understand the[ir] resistance to doing it. So I'm not as impatient with that as I used to be, but it's still real frustrating.

Like Jason, Rosalind revealed her frustration that people of color did not necessarily choose to do their community organizing with *her* [predominantly white] antiracist group. Yet unlike Jason, she expressed some willingness to understand the reasoning behind these African Americans' decisions. Both Jason and Rosalind demonstrate that false empathy is an easy pattern to fall into and that it takes a conscious effort to resist it.

Part of the journey to true empathy for whites is not only facing the historical atrocities committed by whites against people of color, but also realizing that the distrust of whites that people of color may have is grounded in this history. White antiracists who grasp this reality may be more likely to wait out the initial distrust and work toward forming relationships with people of color. Pam explained,

> A white antiracist is looked at very skeptically from the community of color, and *rightfully so*. [They may think:] "Why is this person who has no association with a person of color other than friends, why are they willing to risk this or do that for me?" Until that person, that group, whatever gets to know an individual and understand why [they are antiracist], I think, their skepticism—I can't condemn them for that. If a white person comes around, there's gotta be a reason why they're doing something that they're doing. Why did the army men give all those warm blankets to the Indians, [knowing] that [the blankets] were infected with smallpox? They gave those blankets to those people for a reason, they wanted to get rid of them [the Indians]! So why am I doing something then? Do I wanna get inside so I can find out the inner work-

ings of the community so I can destroy it, or am I a curiosity-seeker, or do I really want to help? So I think people of color should look at white antiracists a little questionably at first and until they realize that this person's OK. They have *every reason* for being skeptical.

While Rosalind stated that she "understand[s] the resistance" of people of color to working with antiracist whites, here Pam elaborated on the source of that resistance, seeming truly empathic. In this case, rather than exhibiting false empathy, Pam spoke from a place of wanting to understand where people of color were coming from, even though in condoning those actions she accepted some treatment of her as a white person ("skepticism") that might have been uncomfortable for her.

In accepting that skepticism toward white antiracists is historically rational, it follows that whites also accept that relationships with people of color may not necessarily occur to the extent that they would like or on the timetable that they would like. Amy recalled how painful it was for her to move toward this kind of acceptance, saying that it began with her transformative women's studies experience:

> When I was able to make the connection between myself and other people being oppressed, then it all turned around. Then I understood issues of separatism and stuff like that, that I never understood before, because then I could see how I would want it. And if I wanted it, then—I remember writing in my journal how sad I was about the fact that I finally understood, because it meant that I would have to [accept that people of color might not want to associate with me]. I was really upset, I was really struggling with the fact that I didn't want people— like some of the people that I loved most in the world were people of color—and I didn't want them to like not want to talk to me, and then it was really hard for me to come to terms with the fact that I would have to say that politically, yes, I agree that if you never want to speak to me again that's really fine. And that was really, really tough.

Although whites who are oppressed in other, nonracialized ways, are not exempt from exhibiting false empathy toward people of color, in Amy's case she was able to use her understanding of feminist politics to develop empathy with even the choices of people of color that would hurt her personally and deeply. Here she drew upon the distinctly female path to empathy called "approximating experiences" discussed in chapter 2. While Jason's "guard went up" to protect him from feeling this kind of rejection from an African American person, Amy allowed herself to explore that feeling of rejection and develop a more macro perspective on it so she would not take it personally. In this sense, we can understand false empathy as a more emotionally "safe" position, since true empathy means potentially opening up to face the kind of pain over which one has no control.

GUARDING AGAINST FALSE EMPATHY: PI'S ACCOUNTABILITY AND AUTHENTIC RELATIONSHIPS

Again, in exploring the organizational resources available for white antiracists struggling to do truly empathic work, PI emerged as having a framework conducive to sustaining this struggle. In a similar vein of Delgado's (1996) discussion of false empathy, PI asserts that well-intentioned white antiracists may be doing more harm than good if they do not have "accountability" to people of color through "authentic relationships" with them. Recall that PI member Mike valued his authentic relationships with people of color because they challenged him when he made excuses for not confronting racism: "Sometimes when I'm interpreting it as, 'I was just trying to—you know, I don't wanna turn 'em off, I have a plan, I'm gonna meet with them for coffee next week'—so you know, it's like, bullshit! You just, you kept your mouth shut, and you let an opportunity go, that kind of thing."

As Mike pointed out, forming authentic relationships with people of color means moving beyond the polite niceties typical of interracial "friendships" in the United States to situations where "bullshit!" might be part of the shared vocabulary. Mike said people of color have helped him to be honest with himself about times when he was not as effective an antiracist as he could have been—when he thought he was doing the best thing for antiracism but was really not. These authentic relationships serve as a checkpoint guarding against the overconfidence that is typical of false empathy.

David, longtime PI organizer and trainer, addressed why the concept of accountability is important for whites.

> There's got to be *accountability* to oppressed peoples. . . . otherwise, even though we [whites] would claim to be antiracist, we'd change the subject. We would, by the very nature of what it means to be white, if all of us get into a room talking, and meeting, and doing whatever, if we're not held *accountable*, the forces will take us off course. And we will either start fighting with each other on the things that white folks fall out with each other on, or we would begin to take over the study of what it means to be white in a way that doesn't mesh with peoples of color's reality.

David made the point that authentic relationships with people of color serve the function of holding whites accountable to the communities they claim to be helping. Accountability cannot be achieved in superficial relationships where the parties involved do not feel comfortable enough to speak candidly without being received defensively or not being heard. As Autonomous as a white antiracist may be, sometimes holding back and listening to how a person of color feels about any given situation can be the most effective course of action.

PI member Kendra described the tenacity and commitment that goes into sustaining authentic relationships, even when being held accountable causes humiliation and pain:

> The first year that I was working in relation to the community I work in [an African American community]. . . . I was very excited about their model of organizing and I wrote two articles about it, and had them published. And I had passed them around the community beforehand, and stuff, but when it came out, [pause] it was a shock to people when I brought these books that had these articles in them, it was a shock to people. And this was not what they expected. And they felt used, and they felt abused, and they felt that their lives had been taken from them and put in a book and by someone they trusted—it really breached the trust that we had very, very deeply. And it was also my first two published articles in my life. So I was just really , just so sad and hurt about that. This was supposed to be my first success, and it was turning out to be my first failure. So I had to sit down with the community, and talk about it. And the people were *really* angry at me, and I made a commitment that I was going to accept responsibility [pause]. And at

the same time, being willing to hear about it and accept responsibility and coming to the table, it didn't make them any less angry, and it didn't heal the trust. . . . But in the last several years I've stayed at the table, and I've continued to work, and I've continued to mess up in other ways, and do things, that they were really pissed at me about, and got my butt kicked. And they haven't blown me off completely. And I know that, in some ways, they like having me around, and maybe [there's] not as much trust as there was initially, but there's more trust than there was when it first happened. . . . What I've learned [from this] is an understanding that, to really make the change happen that needs to happen in this world, it's gonna take commitment and staying in there and hanging in there when things get difficult.

In this instance, Kendra thought she was being accountable, as she consulted "the community beforehand," but was devastated when her actions resulted in a major break of trust between herself and the people of color with whom she worked. She definitely hit the kind of disastrous "mine field" Nancy described in the first words of this chapter. Yet again we see that post-Autonomy is hardly calm and peaceful. However, PI equipped Kendra with an understanding of the importance of the maintenance of these "authentic relationships" which helped her to gradually repair the trust. The PI organization, although institutional in its analysis of racism, does much to assist white antiracists through the emotional challenges of reaching truly empathic antiracist work.

HUMILITY—WHAT "WHITE PEOPLE NEED BIG TIME"

A discussion of humility as a barrier to establishing trust among antiracists is closely related to the discussion of false empathy, since those who are falsely empathic may lack the humility to admit they may not be right. For white antiracists, humility involves a recognition of the inevitability of their making mistakes as a part of their work. It also requires a willingness to learn from those mistakes rather than letting the disappointment they produce drive them to disengage. Mac's comment typified this approach:

So I started trying to be not racist, and was totally unsuccessful at it, and still I am not skilled at it, because you get programmed at an early age and then deprogramming your uncontrollable mental processes as a white person that grew up in this culture—or as a male, for that matter—is not that easy! So this is why it's a lifelong kind of evolution.

Mac accepted that making mistakes and learning from them is a "lifelong" process, and was humble enough to recognize those mistakes. It is easier to be humble if one appreciates the inescapable "minefields" that will occur along the way. Dorothy had a similar perspective.

> I think this pressure to do it all—quote, it's really a trap. And in my own thinking it comes from thinking that I see it all, and I don't see it all, I just see the parts that I'm living anyways. So [the goal is] to try and make the connection that we're all human and we try something and sometimes it doesn't work and we feel like, "ugh I'm never going to try this again." But every moment is new so you can pick yourself up again! And then there'll be another opportunity.

Dorothy's last sentences echoed Mac's long-sighted view that there will be many opportunities throughout one's antiracist life to continue improving upon one's earlier trials and errors—to "regenerate" as a salamander would.

Nancy, who raised the salamander analogy, described lack of humility as a barrier for some whites, but advocated its importance in achieving tenacity as an antiracist:

> There are always going to be explosions in which I'm going to play a role. I'm never going to be good enough at this that I'm not going to cause some injury to myself and others. . . . [You should] accept yourself and think you're good enough to do this work, without having to think you need to be perfect. Because don't you think that stops a lot of white people? [me: yeah] Because we know that we're gonna make mistakes, and we know we're gonna show ourselves to be flawed and that we're gonna cause some hurt. But you have to have the courage to get up every day and do it, knowing that that's true, and I think that's part of what bell [hooks] would call the joy in struggle. I mean, it is struggle! And in struggle you're gonna get hurt, and you're gonna see your weaknesses, but somehow you're gonna find a way to use that vulnerability as another tool.

Being humble means admitting to one's imperfections. According to Nancy (and the others above) imperfection should be seen as a given. She also described struggle as a given, indicating that it will follow throughout an antiracist's life.

We know that activists of color tend to find it easier to work with and trust those white antiracists who are humble. The above quotes demonstrate that humility is not a static quality or personality trait, but rather is a process which is constantly worked at through often difficult and painful emotions. Yet those who are able to maintain humility are more likely to be successful in long-term antiracist struggles.

NAVIGATING MINEFIELDS

Certainly white antiracists face more personal struggles than could possibly be covered in this chapter alone. However, here I have focused on their struggles to move through the stages of racial identity, and also their struggles to achieve true empathy and humility during their continued antiracist work. One of the most interesting steps for white antiracists was the movement out of Pseudo-Independence and into Immersion and Autonomy. In our racialized society, two major stumbling blocks to this process are embedded into the very structure of the system. The first is the construction of racism as a "black problem" in which whites have no business getting involved. Malcolm X gave a speech once where he talked about John Brown and how white society had demonized him as a "nut" so that other whites would be discouraged from following in his antiracist path. Even though whites have always been involved in antiracism, that history, outlined in the beginning of this book, is not a common part of our educational curriculum. As a result, whites sometimes have trouble conceptualizing themselves as being antiracist unless they paint themselves as an "honorary black." Closely related to this issue is the second stumbling block of whites not being able to see themselves as members of a larger racial group. It is easy for whites to dissociate themselves from whiteness without this sense of belonging to a cultural collective. In the absence of this awareness, there is no feeling of responsibility or obligation to give back to one's community by reaching out in an antiracist way to them. Several whites struggled to move past these two stumbling blocks in order to reach "Autonomy"—being comfortably white and antiracist whether in white, nonwhite, or mixed social space.

Beyond this identity development, there is also the daily struggle of remaining humble and being truly empathic to the experiences of people of color in a racist society. White antiracists had to face the hurt and pain of not being trusted in their work. Sometimes this distrust was due to their own actions, and other times it was by no fault of their own but simply due to their membership in this larger historical collective which has historically not lived up to that trust. Those who were able to place these struggles in this historical context were able to "regenerate" after crossing these minefields and continue to do effective antiracist work. Accepting oneself as but a work in progress seemed to be a key in weathering these storms.

As in the chapter on institutional activism, ARA members were relatively absent from this discussion. Again, this can be linked back to their frame of racism and antiracism. Struggling personally with internal issues and personal relationships is not as central when racism is framed as hate groups and abusive police officers. There is little soul-searching to be done when those perpetuating racism are distant entities of which we could rarely see ourselves as a part. Being older and more experienced in activism than most ARA members, Mac was the only exception who really humbled himself in terms of his own racism. For the most part, the ARA members I talked to did not see their own role in racism as a primary concern. In chapter 2, Several ARA members recalled their journeys to becoming antiracist, but the "progressions" discussed in this chapter, which all occurred while the person was already antiracist, were not typical of ARA members. They were less likely to discuss being works-in-progress, perhaps because compared to the targets of their antiracist actions, they were pretty well progressed! It is also important to note that ARA members did not mention any particular aversion to whites which would be typical of Pseudo-Independence. Thus, on a number of levels, the emotional struggles outlined in this chapter were mainly beyond the frame of reference of most ARA members I met.

In contrast, several of the white antiracists who did not identify with either organization shared some of the same struggles that PI members faced. They experienced shifts in their antiracist identities over time as they became more comfortable reaching out to other whites and accepting the inevitability of mistakes, especially in their work with people of color. Although these issues were similar, whether the respondents were in PI or not, PI members had an "analysis" (as they call it in the workshop) that helped them immediately recognize the nature of and deal with their struggles. This can be seen by contrasting the experience of PI member Mike with that of nonmember Nancy. Mike rather promptly recognized that he had isolated himself from whites who had been his "support system," whereas Nancy recalled a process which was over thirty years in the making to get to the same point. This is not to say that PI members are exempt from these struggles, but rather that they have a framework in which to interpret and make sense of them, which may make it easier to sustain them.

What is interesting about this PI framework is that it is grounded in an institutional perspective (racism = prejudice + power) that looks at how systems create racism, yet it still prepares members well for individual emotional challenges. C. Wright Mills (1959) has written that the sociological imagination helps us to see that personal troubles are also public issues, and it may be useful to consider the PI frame of racism as a lens through which members can see their personal troubles. When we are able to see that our personal troubles are not isolated, but rather shared by others who occupy the same social positions, a sense of desperation may be replaced by one of connection to larger society. It also encourages a sense of efficacy, or ability to do something about one's troubles, that might be absent if one felt it was a unique and solitary experience.

This recognition also raises the issue yet again of the importance of building a visible white antiracist community. Whether or not the community in one's immediate environment has the same organizational frame as PI is not as crucial as simply knowing there are others going through the same struggles with whom one can share experiences and to whom one can offer mutual support. That one white antiracist could go decades without any positive white antiracist role models to show her son is an indicator that part of racism is not just keeping people of color in "their place" but also keeping whites in "their place," of maintaining the system without challenging it. There are some whites who believe that the only

way to upset this system is for whites to say they will no longer
participate in the "white club" of privileges, becoming "race traitors" and disrupting the concept of whiteness altogether (Ignatiev
and Garvey 1996). Thus, the concept of a supportive community of
antiracists gathering around a common "white" identity would be
seen as counterproductive under this "race traitor" perspective.
However, there is a pitfall in this approach, because in the absence
of a "white" identity, these race traitors often become "honorary
blacks," perpetuating that Pseudo-Independent experience. There
will be many others who still consider themselves white from
whom race traitors have dissociated, thus reducing their potential
for bringing about antiracist change. Like the Pseudo-Independent
antiracist, they will be largely "preaching to the choir." Ignatiev
and Garvey's *Race Traitor* (1996) is useful in that it adds to the visibility of white antiracist role models, collecting their stories into
one place. Yet a book alone cannot provide a supportive community, especially when it does not advise readers to reach out to
other whites but rather to reach away from whiteness altogether.

In order to sustain the struggles that they are likely to face, white
antiracists need to somehow recognize that these are challenges
unique to their experience of being white and making the conscious choice to daily, vigilantly fight racism. When they are distrusted or criticized, this is not a personal problem unique to them,
but is a result of the historical interaction of whiteness and racism.
Certainly if organizations want to provide them with techniques to
cope with these issues (such as accountability and authentic relationships) this can only help. But simply to have a supportive and
visible community of whites who are proudly antiracist yet simultaneously humble works-in-progress would be a welcome first
step.

NOTES

1. As with most stage theories, a linear progression is not assumed—
people could ostensibly move back and forth between stages, or remain in
one stage indefinitely.

2. The Student Nonviolent Coordinating Committee (SNCC) was a civil

rights organization active in the 1960s which later "reorganized" in the spirit of Black Power and black pride.

3. In other PI workshops, this aspect of white culture has been called "Member-to-Object" (MO) and contrasted with the "Member-to-Group" (MG) culture of blacks and Latinos.

7

THE FUTURE OF ANTIRACISMS

> Understand that relationships and thought processes are fluid, and that what [antiracism] might mean for me today may not be what it means for me in a week. . . . It is an ever changing process.

The above quote is from an African American antiracist. She explained that her conceptualization of how she experiences racism is not static, but "ever changing." Those whites who want to relate to her by memorizing a checklist of "politically correct" things to say and not say to her are missing the point. Rather, she would like them to be open to listening to how she sees racism at any point in time. Just as people of color share many diverse antiracist viewpoints, so too do white antiracists. One white antiracist may hold different philosophies on how she or he should do the work over time. Moreover, different white antiracists may have different ways for approaching the same problem, or even may be focusing on different problems altogether. In the absence of a uniform agenda, can white antiracists come together across state lines and communities to form a more visible presence? Is this even a desirable goal?

Two major antiracist organizations share the common goal of fighting racism. They share the goal of wanting to involve more and more people in their struggles, and just by being active in their communities they have done so. Their white members share passions about wanting to reduce the daily assaults on the humanity of other members of our society. Yet they differ on nearly every-

thing else. From where they focus their efforts to even the definition of racism itself, in some ways they are as opposite as night
and day. This makes it increasingly difficult to visualize a unified
antiracist movement toward which aspiring white antiracists can
look. Since white antiracists are few and far between as it is, the
lack of a common language among them poses a challenge for any
quest for complete unity. However, there is potential for coalition
building among these groups as well as among those who do not
have access to any such group in their immediate surroundings.
The key to this potential lies in defining racism as broadly as possible, even as the differences between white antiracists lie in how
they define racism. Competing frames of racism separate the two
organizations, yet fitting each of these frames into a larger frame
of which they each hold a part opens up possibilities in which all
white antiracists, regardless of organizational affiliation (or lack
thereof) can be included.

STRENGTHS THAT ORGANIZATIONS SHARE

Although in some ways as different as night and day, ARA and PI
do both provide some similar resources to members. For one thing,
they both make antiracism a visible option in their communities,
regardless of what form that antiracism takes. Several of the activists I interviewed stressed ARA or PI "recruitment" (for lack of a
better word) as crucial to their becoming antiracists in the first
place. For example, Jason began going to ARA meetings with a
friend. Ani picked up some literature about ARA and its meeting
time at a local concert, and then attended as part of a course assign-
ment to participate in a social movement. Holly embarked upon a
trial-and-error search for someplace to be an activist when she finally settled on ARA, which was well publicized in her area. Pam,
Rosalind, Henry, and Mike all attended the PI Undoing Racism
workshop on the recommendation of friends. None of these individuals had any strong commitments to antiracism before their
involvement with these groups. This lends support to the argument that more whites would become antiracist if only they just

knew where to go or what to do. Organizations thus serve as these "role model" examples.

Additionally, regardless of its frame of racism, being a member of a local organization appears to protect white antiracists from job- or life-threatening repercussions for their work. Recall from chapter 5 that all of the examples of "occupational hazards"— white antiracists penalized in some way for their actions—were told by individuals who, at the time of the incident, were not affiliated with any particular antiracist organization. Certainly, it is easier for those who wish to penalize antiracists to direct their disapproval at a single individual rather than a group. But we also must consider the organization as a supportive resource for planning successful actions. For example, if Amy had consulted a larger group about how to respond to the racist fraternity at her school, they might have advised her not to put her name and home phone number on the signs; ARA encourages chapters to use post office boxes as contact information rather than home addresses or numbers precisely for this reason. If she had worked in conjunction with ARA for this action, undoubtedly they would have alerted her to this fact and saved her from threatening phone calls. Similarly, when David made the decision to take his students to a civil rights demonstration, if he had consulted a group like PI first, they might have first asked him who else at the school might be supportive, and advised him to act in conjunction with these individuals or with certain community groups. Then he might have been less likely to have been isolated and fired. Organizations serve as a contact point, especially for new activists, to connect with more veteran activists on what works and what does not work. This expertise and foresight contributes to the buffer effect that organizations have in protecting against the more serious "occupational hazards" of antiracism.

The recruitment potential and the "safety effect" of both ARA and PI were the most notable similarities between the two. Again, it is also evident that both groups share a passion for organizing against the atrocious effects that racism has on society, perhaps the most important and crucial concurrence. What the organizations share in common is important to keep in mind, because sometimes the differences seem almost overwhelming.

DIFFERENT FRAMES, DIFFERENT PICTURES

The different frames that ARA and PI use to define racism were made evident throughout this text, so I will summarize them only briefly. ARA focuses on "hate in any form" and targets mainly neo-Nazi groups, the Ku Klux Klan, and police brutality in terms of their organizing efforts. PI defines racism as "race prejudice plus power" and targets everyday institutions such as school and government in their organizing efforts. These overall organizing frames result in several practical differences between the two groups. Although both groups do well at "recruiting" new members, it is interesting to note how the competing frames result in differences even here. ARA seems more focused on raising the sheer numbers of ARA members and is not as concerned about educating them into any particular framework, provided they agree to the four principles (listed in chapter 1). On the other hand, PI sees their two-and-one-half-day Undoing Racism workshop as crucial, because they claim there are many people who may think they are antiracist but are actually doing more harm than good in the communities where they think they are helping. If forced to choose between two hundred people who have not done their workshop but want to help their community and twenty people who still want to help *and* have done the workshop, they may go with the latter since there would be no way of guaranteeing that the former would not simply result in more damage to the community. In table 7.1, I have summarized this difference as quantity versus quality, noting simply what is *most* important to each. Ideally, of course, both would prefer quantity *and* quality of membership, but the frame dictates on what they will spend more time and energy. ARA spends a lot of time tabling (collecting names) and PI spends a lot of time holding workshops (educating).

The way ARA and PI have framed antiracism also affects how members see race itself, in terms of how they claim to perceive themselves and people of color. PI members tend to be *reflexively* race cognizant, whereas ARA members tend to be *selectively* race cognizant. This means that PI members are explicit about noticing their own race and a person of color's race, while ARA members recognize how "racists" use race as a way of dispensing power and privilege but strive not to notice race in their own interactions. In

Table 7.1 Similarities and Differences between Antiracist Organizations

	PI	ARA	Both Organizations
Becoming involved	Quality of "recruits" paramount	Quantity of "recruits" paramount	Provide visible place to start; recruitment when friends ask others to join
Frame of racism	Covert racism perpetuated by members of everyday institutions; reflexive race cognizance	Overt racism perpetuated by hate groups and police; selective race cognizance	
Individual actions	More likely to use long-term strategy of building relationship with perpetrator; "maintain relationships"	More likely to confront head-on	
Institutional actions	Use own positions within institutions to bring about change; "gatekeepers"	Challenge institutions in which they are not members, such as the police	Provide buffer against repercussions; less likely to have individual jobs/lives threatened
Emotional struggles	Provide context within which to interpret distrust; "authentic relationships"; "accountability"	Personal struggles and relationships not a primary focus	

this respect, it is as if the two groups are speaking different languages. For ARA members, colorblindness is a desired goal for all, while for PI members, colorblindness is described as "denial" and even as a form of racism itself. This is hardly a matter of semantics since it has everything to do with their organizing efforts. To ARA members, prejudice in any form is the target, and the race of the perpetrator is of no concern. As Travis put it, racists come in "every color and every nationality." Further, the members' own racial backgrounds matter little in how they organize. While ARA is predominantly white, it does have members of color, but no difference is articulated about how those members should proceed in terms of their actions. The guidelines for protesting and issues one will face as an antiracist are not separated out by race. This contrasts with PI, which has a separate group for whites called European Dissent and stresses that the issues whites face and people of color face when doing antiracism are very different. Being reflexive, PI members also speak about working on their "own racism," as distinct from ARA members who focus on the "hatemongers" (which do not include themselves).

This focus on their "own racism" on the part of PI bespeaks humility, and this has an outcome on how they react to racism at the individual level. Perhaps because they see themselves as not so far removed from anyone who could make a racist comment or joke, PI members tend to take actions that will result in befriending that person rather than insulting him or her. ARA member Holly felt free to boldly call individuals out on a streetcar, perhaps because she saw them as "hatemongers" of which she did not feel a part. In contrast, PI members are taught to "maintain relationships" with other white people, and to see themselves as part of a "white collective" (another reflexive outlook). Thus, they are more likely to formulate long-term strategies for developing a relationship with the perpetrator of a racist comment or joke, in hopes of persuading the person to think about it differently, and maybe even to come to a workshop.

Again, being reflexively race cognizant allows whites to see themselves as participants in racism in a way that being selectively race cognizant would not. As such, when focusing on institutional racism, PI members struggle to bring change into the institutions where they live, work, and worship, while ARA members challenge institutions such as the police force, which they explicitly advocate in their principles should not be considered *allies,* much less should ARA members consider *being* police officers. In evaluating their successes, then, it is notable that PI members tend to stress changes in their own institutions (adding "antiracist" to Kendra's church mission statement; adding a multicultural arts program to Pam's school) while ARA members point to high attendance at protest events as a success. The latter perspective not only emphasizes resistance against an entity of which one is not a member (for example, the KKK), but it also reminds us of the focus on quantity as opposed to quality.

Finally, being reflexive means that personal struggles with emotions and relationships are much more of a concern. I never asked my respondents to talk about feelings specifically, so the fact that PI members brought emotions up more regularly into our discussions indicates that they see emotions as more of a part of antiracism than do ARA members. Further, PI members relied on specific terminology such as accountability and authentic relationships when describing these personal struggles, so even the terminology itself invites PI members to reflect on their own personal relationships as a part of antiracism. This focus on terminology brings us back to a key point: that these two organizations sometimes may as well be speaking different languages.

NONORGANIZATIONAL MEMBERS: MORE LIKE PI THAN ARA

Many of the voices I have drawn upon in this analysis were not members of ARA or PI, so I would be remiss in omitting them from this discussion. It became evident throughout the analysis here that those who were not affiliated with either ARA or PI were more likely to be reflexively than selectively race cognizant. Even though their journey to that point might have been self-described as longer than that of PI members, most had made it there by the time our interview took place. The similarity of those who were not exposed to PI's philosophy to PI members themselves can only be explained by examining the different frames involved.

PI's and ARA's different frames of who is the antagonist, and where one's actions should be directed, have everything to do with why individuals acting alone are less likely to model ARA's selective race cognizance. Framing racism as part of everyday institutions (as does reflexive race cognizance) means it is easier for whites to participate in the absence of an organization; challenging a group like neo-Nazis is less inviting of a task to take on by oneself. Even though institutions are seen as larger than life, and neo-Nazis seen as isolated crazies, in reality neo-Nazis seldom practice in isolation. They recruit members just like ARA or PI does, by encouraging friends of the virtues of the group. Thus, a single individual who wishes to counterdemonstrate against neo-Nazis or KKK members finds himself or herself up against a pack of people for which she or he is no match. Further, one actually has to research when a right-wing group is going to demonstrate, or else rely upon an antiracist group for information on when they think the group will demonstrate. This again places emphasis on the group, whereas people are always at their job, church, school, or home and can regularly observe racism in those areas without consulting others. Although a group might help advise individuals on how to challenge that racism in those areas without ending up threatened or fired, there are many less risky things one can do in those settings without needing the backing of a group. Therefore, the very nature of being an isolated antiracist lends itself to being reflexive about one's involvement in racism, hence the closer resemblance to PI's reflexively race cognizant frame.

SAME FRAME, DIFFERENT PICTURES

While throughout this work I have used the social movements concept of framing, it will be useful when considering the future of antiracism to think literally of frames and pictures for the sake of analogy. There is one style of picture frame that allows for two or three or more pictures to be put in it, due to the way the matting is cut. These are sometimes referred to as collage frames. It is this type of frame that I will use as my analogy to discuss the possibility of coalition building between multiple antiracist groups that is necessary if we are to ever see a strong white antiracist presence in our society.

The discrepant frames between ARA and PI are directly related to how they define racism. ARA says racists are other, hateful people, while PI says racists are all whites since institutions lean toward privileging them. Due to the inclusion of all whites in the latter definition, white PI members posit themselves in that definition. All the differences in organizing tactics and foci of energy then flow from those competing frames. If ARA members talked about being colorblind, PI members would see them as racist, while if PI members said all whites are racist and people of color cannot be racist, ARA would find this in itself to be a racist and prejudicial statement. Although my research did not involve members of the two groups directly dialoging about the other's frame of racism, disagreements were directly implicated in many of their respective statements. With these two diametrically opposing frames, the outlook for coalition building between the two groups seems pessimistic, to say the least.

However, if frames of antiracism are based on one's definition of racism, let us conceptualize a definition within which both groups could work inside the same frame. Racism is a system of advantage for those of the privileged "race" (which would be whites in the context of the United States) which has both overt and covert manifestations and occurs at both individual and institutional levels. Within this all-inclusive definition, it is evident that all of the white antiracists interviewed for this study are at least working on *some* aspect of racism. This is an important point, since there are those who may argue that anyone who says they do not notice their own race, or that of others, cannot truly be antiracist. They may question whether some ARA members are actually antiracist, if they are focusing only on overt acts of prejudice. However, since racism is maintained through a combination of overt and covert acts, and through a combination of individual and institutional levels, to say that ARA is an antiprejudice, but not an antiracist, group is incorrect. They do indeed focus on *part* of racism. Indeed it would be impossible to focus on every aspect of racism simultaneously. It is a multifaceted problem, to be sure.

Yet it is unclear whether ARA subscribes to this definition, and is just choosing to focus on one aspect for the sake of practicality, or whether its members are guided by a limited view of racism. If we examine the only four principles that all ARA chapters must

agree to (see full text in chapter 1), they begin with the commitment to publicly challenge "racists/fascists" whenever they are organizing in public. "We go where they go," it reads. Are the only
racists those who stand on a street corner and proclaim their prejudices unabashedly? The second and third principles refer to using
grassroots tactics and agreeing to disagree among chapters, so it is
not until the fourth and final principle that we see an actual broad-
ening of focus. The fourth principle mentions "discrimination,"
but this word is immediately followed by "against the disabled,
the oldest, the youngest and the weakest of our society." Thus, this
alerts us to a wider range of "isms" than just racism, but it does not
necessarily point to a broader conceptualization of racism itself.

Notably, the *ARA News* edition circulated by the Columbus,
Ohio, chapter features clippings of newspaper articles highlighting
various forms of discrimination, including job-based civil rights
lawsuits like a black fast-food worker being fired because of her
braids. Mac was responsible for collecting these articles. It is evident from the excerpts of Mac's interview that Mac had a different
perspective than most ARA members. He was considerably older,
having lived through the civil rights movement, and he was reflexive in terms of thinking about his own role in racism in a way that
other ARA members were not. Mac attempted to infuse a more
inclusive definition of racism into this particular publication, but
my interviews with other ARA members did not clearly indicate
that anyone else had picked up on this wider perspective. All of
the articles in *ARA News* which highlighted activism focused on
the efforts of Copwatch or on neo-Nazi groups. While Mac's approach of getting members' "foot-in-the-door" and educating
them later may have its advantages in terms of *quantity* of membership, members may be left with limited understandings of racism
that will not help them to see it when it is going on in their midst
(including when they themselves are the culprits).

Conversely, PI members may not often focus on "hate groups,"
but they recognize they are one aspect of racism at least. The European Dissent press conference about the racist fraternity (discussed
in chapter 5) was one of the rare times that PI members focused on
overt racist acts. For the most part, they do their antiracist work
within their own places of work and worship, usually focusing on
more covert dimensions of racism. However, the educational as-

pect of PI provided by the Undoing Racism workshop allows for racism to actually be defined for members in a way that is never done by ARA. This meant that everyone I interviewed from PI gave me similar definitions of racism when asked, but ARA members each presented their own unique definition. Travis focused on "hate-mongering," while Tim also mentioned "outward hatred" but then admitted there were more subtle things like the internal discomfort he sometimes got around people of color since he so rarely sees them where he lives. So ARA members differed in the degree to which they included covert aspects of racism, while PI members were unanimous about racism having multiple manifestations. The white antiracists who were not members of either group provided definitions similar to those given by PI members. They consistently included "unintentional" (covert) aspects of racism like white privilege in their definitions in a way that ARA members did not. In our society, we often agree that something is racist if it is overt, yet we have a harder time agreeing upon the less overt manifestations of racism. This disagreement is no less present among the white antiracists featured in this study.

Keeping the all-encompassing definition of racism as an overarching frame, there could be room for certain antiracist groups to work on overt hate groups while others work on covert racism in less public settings. That is, within the frame of racism, particular antiracist groups could focus on different issues within this frame. Yet this is not exactly what is happening on the current antiracist scene. Instead, there is a lack of agreement upon the definition of racism, so some antiracists are taking a myopic view and not even realizing that they are working on but one piece of a much larger puzzle. I discussed in chapter 3 how selective race cognizance can be used as a strategy—that is, language which reflects this myopic view of racism (e.g., colorblindness) could be used as a tool to engage mainstream whites with antiracism as an initial step. However, when antiracists continue to conceptualize racism as mainly overt acts only, even after some time with an antiracist organization, it becomes less plausible to regard the limited frame as solely strategic. Acknowledging all facets of racism while strategically directing tactics at one aspect of it is quite different from directing tactics at one aspect of racism while ignoring its other manifestations. In order for these antiracists to be working within the same frame with their different tactics, those who focus on overt acts would have to be cognizant of their own role in racist institutions even if that is not where they chose to direct their antiracist energies. If these changes were made, coalition building among white antiracists would be a more foreseeable part of the future of antiracism.

This is not to suggest that all social movement organizations within a movement should share a common ideology. Indeed, this has never been the case with any social justice movement. Historically, such organizations have ranged from the most liberal to the most radical within almost any movement, from civil rights and feminism to environmental and labor movements. Organizations have combined forces, tackling different aspects of the problem, and often vehemently disagreeing with each other on whose area of focus is more necessary. However, when we consider the situation of white antiracists, their organizational rifts present a more serious challenge than mere *tactical* differences, because *framing* differences between white antiracists revolve around how they define their *own* relationship to the problem. African Americans may find themselves disagreeing on whether to use violent or nonviolent tactics, for example, but they are less likely to disagree on the fundamental issue of whether they are impacted by racism themselves. Following the frame and picture analogy, they would be working within the same definitional frame of the problem but selecting different areas of focus or different pictures within the frame. This is the most common type of difference we see historically between social movement organizations. The framing issue is particularly central for white antiracists precisely because they are privileged resistors—they stand to benefit from racism in ways their allies of color do not. Therefore, working in different frames altogether comes out of whites' struggle with conceptualizing their own role in racism. While in any social movement there is undoubtedly room for disagreement about where one's energies are best focused, coalition building would be enhanced if there were minimal agreement on the frame of the problem, particularly members' own relationship to it.

WHAT WHITES CAN DO ABOUT RACISM

Ideally, coalition building would be so successful that there would be visible antiracist groups with sizable white involvement in nearly every community. Yet this vision is undoubtedly futuristic, perhaps distantly so. Immediately, however, there are still many ways whites can become active in fighting racism, and the data presented here attest to those multiple possibilities. While those possibilities are endless, they can be summarized in three key areas: finding strength in numbers, strategizing actions for maximum effectiveness, and striving for humility.

Finding Strength in Numbers

We know that the most effective antiracist actions have not occurred in isolation. There are many antiracist organizations across the United States and Canada in which whites can take part. (A partial list appears in Appendix A). If available, whites can get involved with a local organization. Membership grows by member referral. White antiracists should remind themselves that part of their antiracist work includes reaching out to others, particularly other whites, so inviting others to meetings and workshops with their organization would be a crucial way of extending this work. Also, white antiracists may want to be proactive in seeing to it that their organization is aware of all manifestations of racism, both overt and covert, and make sure white members are mindful of the ways in which they participate in racism themselves from day to day.

White antiracists can also find strength in numbers even outside of any antiracist organization. If they are interested in fighting racism in the areas where they live and work, they should talk to others in those areas who they think might be sympathetic to such work. This kind of networking may include passing on particularly influential readings or other forms of expression which could be influential in making those other people aware of the reality of modern racism and its effects, if they are not already aware. Again, one undertakes this work cognizant of overt and covert levels of racism. Certainly, if racism is manifesting itself overtly in one's home community, there are readily visible places to begin. However, there are many other necessary tasks for white antiracists to take on, even in seemingly benign areas. Is there token integration, no integration, or integration at a surface level while covert racism lurks below the surface? We know that some antiracists have begun their work with these very questions about their churches, work-places, gyms, and even their own families. The key in addressing all these issues is to not go at it alone. Transforming these institutions requires the complicity of more than just one of their members. Developing a cadre of allies will be a necessary first step.

Strategizing Actions for Maximum Effectiveness

At both individual and institutional levels, we have seen that white antiracists can make a difference. Clearly, taking antiracist action goes far beyond merely having good intentions. White antiracists most often develop some kind of strategy whereby change would be most likely to occur, keeping in mind that change is not immediate nor should it be postponed indefinitely, whether out of fear or out of privilege. Privileged resistance means that whites have a wider range of options to choose from for fighting racism than people of color do. They are more likely to be seen, heard, and believed, and less likely to suffer repercussions for their actions. With this wider range of choices also comes responsibilities. Several white antiracists have learned through decades of experience that effective action requires a balance between (1) courage to speak out in difficult situations and (2) diplomacy enough to maintain relationships with those in whom change is desired. Effective antiracist action should not result in severing ties with either individuals or institutions who could be sources of antiracist change. By the same token, one should not be so preoccupied with pleasing everyone that no action is ever taken. Simply put, diplomacy should not be confused with complacency. Each situation an antiracist encounters will have to be evaluated, since what constitutes effectiveness in one setting may not be in another. Regardless of the situational specifics, however, keeping away from the two extreme poles of complacency and of aggressively alienating others is the key to developing effective white antiracist strategies.

Striving for Humility

Even when white antiracists gather in large numbers, and strategize for maximum effectiveness, they will undoubtedly make mistakes and in some cases even cause more harm than good. Those white antiracists who recognize the inevitability of these "minefields" that they will face along the way will be more apt to sustain their commitment to antiracism and continue their work despite these setbacks. There is no room for an "ego" in white antiracist work. Whites undergo socialization from birth, which prepares them to effectively uphold the racial status quo and which alone cannot immediately chip these layers of socialization away. The sooner white antiracists accept the lifetime of learning that is ahead of them, the easier it will be for them to be open to criticism and self-improvement, without defensiveness or deflection onto others. As one activist of color put it, "humility is something white people need, big time!" Having white antiracists striving to be humble is crucial in maintaining the commitment to antiracism over the long haul that will be needed in order to incorporate succeeding generations into the process.

Humility with respect to antiracism is especially a challenge because of the individualistic society in which we live. Individualism places emphasis on the ability to control one's own fate. Whites may feel a loss of that sense of control to which they have become accustomed when even their best laid plans come under scrutiny. However, it is important to recognize that we have all inherited a system of racism which was laid in place well before our time. Those white antiracists who are able to maintain humility without defensiveness understand that whatever racial perspectives they have internalized which may end up being responsible for their mistakes originated from the workings of that historical system and not from a personal character flaw. While they do not personalize the *origins* of their mistakes, they still take personal responsibility for learning from them and striving not to repeat them. No matter how many years they have been working at it, truly humble white antiracists acknowledge they have a lifetime of "minefields" ahead. As Lisa stated, "It's taken hundreds of years for this system to be put in place, and you can't fix it in thirty years or even sixty years . . . this just takes a long time, this is a lifetime commitment."

APPENDIX A
CONTACT INFORMATION FOR
ANTIRACIST GROUPS

Here I have included contact information for the most stable and well-established chapters of the groups that I researched for this project. The persons you reach through these contacts will be well-informed about antiracist organizing throughout the United States and Canada, and can most likely refer you to like-minded contacts in your area.

Anti-Racist Action
P.O. Box 10797
Columbus, OH 43201
(614) ACT-MUCH (228-6824); aracolumbus@hotmail.com

Anti-Racist Action
P.O. Box 291, Station B
Toronto, Ontario M5T 2T2
CANADA
(416) 631-8835; ara@web.net

The People's Institute for Survival and Beyond
1444 North Johnson Street
New Orleans, LA 70116-1767
(504) 944-2354; pisabnola@aol.com

APPENDIX B
PROFILE OF RESPONDENTS

Name[a]	Gender	Organization	Age Group	Profile
Amy (DeLorenzo)	Female	None/other	21–30	Protested against racist frat and received death threats; lesbian feminism and antiwar protestor
Angela (Guidice)	Female	None/other[b]	41–50	On senior staff of Visions, Inc. (oppression and social change training); black female partner and biracial son
Ani	Female	ARA	18–20	ARA activist; Jewish
Bob (Woodrick)	Male	None/other	61–70	CEO of DandW foods (grocery stores); gives speeches on racism; namesake of Woodrick Institute for Study of Racism and Diversity
Chester (Hartman)	Male	None/other	61–70	President and Executive Director of Poverty and Race Research Action Council
David (Billings)	Male	PI	51–60	Leads Undoing Racism training; arrested and expelled from Ole Miss in 1960s; ED[c] founder and member
Dorothy (Friesen)	Female	None/other	41–50	Lives in black neighborhood; leads training for whites; writer
Elizabeth	Female	None/other	21–30	Teaches and studies race relations
Harriet (Ludwig)	Female	None/other	80 +	Marched and arrested w/MLK in Selma; fair housing in Chicago; reporter in South exposing racism; welfare rights/education activism
Henry	Male	PI	51–60	ED[a] member; Americorps coordinator and pastor

Name[a]	Gender	Organization	Age Group	Profile
Holly	Female	ARA	21–30	Leads local ARA; Native people's rights, "anticop" organizing
Jack (Donovan)	Male	None/other	51–60	Unitarian minister; working on facing racism within church
Jason	Male	ARA	21–30	ARA internet coordinator; active in Copwatch
Joel (Olson)	Male	None/other	31–40	"New abolitionist"; edits journal of same name
Kendra	Female	PI	31–40	Leads Undoing Racism training; black husband; ED[a] member; antiracist education at church
Kristin	Female	None/other	21–30	Student protestor; worked for racial fairness in justice system
Lisa	Female	PI	21–30	Works for PI; ED[a] member
Mac (Jim MacNamara)	Male	ARA	41–50	ARA organizer and writer; police misconduct litigator
Mark	Male	None/other	41–50	"New abolitionist"; edits *Race Traitor* journal and book
Mike	Male	PI	31–40	Teacher; ED[a] member; organizes PI's Youth Agenda
Nancy (Collins)	Female	None/other	51–60	Race relations facilitator; won award from black college for outstanding race relations work
Olivia (Flak)	Female	ARA	21–30	ARA activist; bisexual; feminist and environmental work
Pam	Female	PI	21–30	Teacher; ED[a] member; instituted multicultural art program at school
Paul (Marcus)	Male	None/other	31–40	Codirector of Community Change (institutional racism is focus); teacher
Pierce (Butler)	Male	None/other	41–50	Anti-KKK demonstrator; active with clinic defense
Rosalind	Female	PI	51–60	ED[a] member; put Undoing Racism training into church and workplace
Scott	Male	None/other	31–40	Student activist; Mexican wife and children

continued

Name[a]	Gender	Organization	Age Group	Profile
Susan	Female	None/other	31–40	Studied antiracism; cofounder of First Circle (antiracist training organization)
Tim	Male	ARA	18–20	Anarchist; led protest against a "white power hour" local TV show
Travis	Male	ARA	31–40	Punk musician; writes antiracist songs; anti-Nazi street activist

[a]Name given is a pseudonym unless a last name appears in parentheses—then it is the person's real name.
[b]If they are not a member of ARA or PI, then "none/other" is listed. This means they are not affiliated with an organization profiled in this text, although they may be members of other organizations. All information current from time of interview (interviews done 1996–1999).
[c]European Dissent

Note on geographic regions of respondents: Although two interviewees resided in Toronto at the time of the interview (both ARA members) and two resided west of the Mississippi River (in North Dakota and Arizona), the rest of the sample, which is a large majority, reside east of the Mississippi River in the United States. Nine lived in the Midwest (Ohio, Illinois, and Michigan); five lived in the Northeast (Massachusetts, New York, and Washington. D.C.); five lived in the Southeast (Florida and North Carolina); and seven lived in Louisiana (all seven were PI members).

REFERENCES

Aptheker, Herbert. 1992. *Antiracism in U.S. History: The First Two Hundred Years.* New York: Greenwood.

Barndt, Joseph. 1991. *Dismantling Racism: The Continuing Challenge to White America.* Minneapolis, Minn.: Augsberg Fortress.

Blauner, Bob. 1995. White Radicals, White Liberals, and White People: Rebuilding the Anti-Racist Coalition. In *Racism and Anti-Racism in World Perspective.* Edited by Benjamin P. Bowser. Thousand Oaks, Calif.: Sage.

Bonilla-Silva, Eduardo. 1997. Rethinking Racism: Toward a Structural Interpretation. *American Sociological Review* 62:465–480.

Carmichael, Stokely, and Charles Hamilton. 1967. *Black Power.* New York: Vintage Books.

Carr, Leslie. 1997. *Colorblind Racism.* Thousand Oaks, Calif.: Sage Publications.

Chisom, Ronald, and Michael Washington. 1997. *Undoing Racism: A Philosophy of International Social Change,* 2nd ed. New Orleans: The People's Institute Press.

Delgado, Richard. 1996. *The Coming Race War?* New York: New York University Press.

Della Dora, Delmo. 1970. *What Curriculum Leaders Can Do About Racism.* Detroit: New Detroit.

Denzin, Norm. 1989. *Interpretive Biography.* Newbury Park, Calif.: Sage Publications.

D'Souza, Dinesh. 1995. *The End of Racism.* New York: The Free Press.

DuBois, W. E. B. [1903] 1965. The Souls of Black Folk. In *Three Negro Classics.* New York: Avon Books.

Eichstedt, Jennifer L. 1997. White Identities and Anti-Racism Activism. Paper presented at the annual meeting of the American Sociological Association, August, Toronto, Ontario.

Essed, Philomena. 1991. *Understanding Everyday Racism*. Thousand Oaks, Calif.: Sage.

Evans, Sara. 1980. *Personal Politics: The Roots of Women's Liberation in the Civil Rights Movement and the New Left*. New York: Vintage.

Feagin, Joe R. 1991. The Continuing Significance of Race: Antiblack Discrimination in Public Places. *American Sociological Review* 56:101–116.

Feagin, Joe R. 2000. *Racist America: Roots, Current Realities, and Future Reparations*. New York: Routledge.

Feagin, Joe R., and Hernán Vera. 1995. *White Racism: The Basics*. New York: Routledge.

Feagin, Joe R., and Melvin P. Sikes. 1994. *Living with Racism: The Black Middle Class Experience*. Boston: Beacon Press.

Fine, Michelle, Lois Weis, Linda C. Powell, and L. Mun Wong. 1997. *Off White: Readings on Race, Power and Society*. New York: Routledge.

Frankenberg, Ruth. 1993. *White Women, Race Matters: The Social Construction of Whiteness*. Minneapolis, Minn.: University of Minnesota Press.

Franklin, Jonathan. 1998. Skinnin' Heads. *Vibe* (June–July): 84–85.

Gilligan, Carol. 1982. *In a Different Voice: Psychological Theory and Women's Development*. Cambridge, Mass.: Harvard University Press.

Greeno, Catherine G., and Eleanor E. Maccoby. 1986. How Different is the "Different Voice"? *Signs* 11:310–316.

Gubrium, Jaber F., and James A. Holstein. 1997. *The New Language of Qualitative Method*. New York: Oxford University Press.

Helms, Janet E., ed. 1990. *Black and White Racial Identity: Theory, Research, and Practice*. New York: Greenwood.

Heritage, John. 1984. *Garfinkel and Ethnomethodology*. Cambridge: Polity Press.

Hill, Mike, ed. 1997. *Whiteness: A Critical Reader*. New York: New York University Press.

Hogan, Tiffany L., and Julie K. Netzer. 1993. "Knowing the Other: White Women, Gender, and Racism." Paper presented at the annual meetings of the American Sociological Association, August, Miami Beach, Florida.

hooks, bell. 1995. *Killing Rage: Ending Racism*. New York: Henry Holt.

Hunt, Scott A., Robert D. Benford, and David A. Snow. 1994. Identity Fields: Framing Processes and the Construction of Social Identities. In *New Social Movements: From Ideology to Identity*. Edited by Enrique Laraña, Hank Johnston, and Joseph R. Gusfield. Philadelphia: Temple University Press.

Ignatiev, Noel, and John Garvey, eds. 1996. *Race Traitor*. New York: Routledge.

Jones, James M., and Robert T. Carter. 1996. Racism and White Racial Identity: Merging Realities. In *Impacts of Racism on White Americans*. Edited by Benjamin P. Bowser and Raymond G. Hunt. Thousand Oaks, Calif.: Sage.

Lewis, Amanda. 1999. There is No Race in the Schoolyard: Colorblind Ideology in An (Almost) All White School. Paper presented at the annual meeting of the American Sociological Association, August 7, Chicago.

Lubiano, Wahneema, ed. 1998. *The House That Race Built*. New York: Vintage.

Massey, Douglas S., and Nancy A. Denton. 1992. *American Apartheid: Segregation and the Making of the Underclass*. Cambridge, Mass.: Harvard University Press.

McAdam, Doug. 1988. *Freedom Summer*. New York: Oxford University Press.

McIntosh, Peggy. 1998. White privilege and male privilege. In *Race, Class, and Gender: An Anthology*, 3rd ed. Edited by Margaret L. Andersen and Patricia Hill Collins. New York: Wadsworth.

Mills, C. Wright. 1959. *The Sociological Imagination*. New York: Oxford University Press.

Novick, Michael. 1997. Anti-Racist Action on the Move. *Turning the Tide: Journal of Anti-Racist Activism Research and Education* 10, no. 2:1–2.

Page, Clarence. 1997. *Showing My Color: Impolite Essays on Race and Identity*. New York: HarperCollins.

Pinkney, Alphonso. 1968. *The Committed: White Activists in the Civil Rights Movement*. New Haven: College and University Press.

Platt, Gerald M., and Michael R. Fraser. 1998. Race and Gender Discourse Strategies: Creating Solidarity and Framing the Civil Rights Movement. *Social Problems* 45:160–179.

Polletta, Francesca. 1998. "It Was Like a Fever . . .": Narrative and Identity in Social Protest. *Social Problems* 45:137–159.

Selena and Katrina. 1996. Copwatch. *Race Traitor* 6:18–23.

Snow, David A., and Robert D. Benford. 1992. Master Frames and Cycles of Protest. In *Frontiers in Social Movement Theory*. Edited by Aldon D. Morris and Carol McClurg Mueller. New Haven: Yale University Press.

Steinhorn, Leonard, and Barbara Diggs-Brown. 2000. *By the Color of Our Skin: The Illusion of Integration and the Reality of Race*. New York: Plume.

Tatum, Beverly Daniel. 1992. Talking About Race, Learning About Racism: The Application of Racial Identity Development Theory in the Classroom. *Harvard Educational Review* 62:1–24.

Tatum, Beverly Daniel. 1994. Teaching White Students About Racism: The Search for White Allies and the Restoration of Hope. *Teachers College Record* 95:462–476.

Tatum, Beverly Daniel. 1997. *Why Are All the Black Kids Sitting Together in the Cafeteria?* New York: Basic Books.

Thomas, Richard W. 1996. *Understanding Interracial Unity*. Thousand Oaks, Calif.: Sage.

Thompson, Becky, and White Women Challenging Racism. 1997. Home/

work: Antiracism and the Meaning of Whiteness. In *Off White: Readings on Race, Power, and Society.* Edited by Michelle Fine, Lois Weis, Linda C. Powell, and L. Mun Wong. New York: Routledge.

Van Dijk, Teun. 1987. *Communicating Racism.* Thousand Oaks, Calif.: Sage.

X, Malcolm. 1965. *The Autobiography of Malcolm X.* New York: Grove.

Index